S0-ARJ-349

COPING
W H E N

A Parent

Is Gay

Deborah A. Miller, Ph.D.

THE ROSEN PUBLISHING GROUP, INC./NEW YORK

Published in 1993 by The Rosen Publishing Group, Inc.
29 East 21st Street, New York, NY 10010

First Edition
Copyright 1993 by Deborah A. Miller

Library of Congress Cataloging-in-Publication Data

Miller, Deborah A.
  Coping when a parent is gay / Deborah A. Miller. — 1st ed.
     p.   cm.
  Includes bibliographical references and index.
  Summary: Examines the impact of a parent's sexual orientation
on family relationships, describing the experiences of young
people in various types of families.
  ISBN 0-8239-1404-6
  1. Gay parents—United States—Juvenile literature.
  2. Children of gay parents—United States—Juvenile literature.
  [1. Gay parents. 2. Parent and child. 3. Family.
  4. Homosexuality.] I. Title
  HQ777.8.M55 1993
  306.874—dc20   92-35878
                                                        CIP
                                                         AC

Manufactured in the United States of America

ABOUT THE AUTHOR ◇

Deborah Miller is an Associate Professor and Health Coordinator of the College of Charleston, Charleston, South Carolina. Her specialty is human sexuality, and she teaches at both the under-graduate and graduate levels. One of her strong points is relaying to teachers ways to facilitate classroom discussions on sensitive issues.

Dr. Miller has published over fifteen research articles, written a student workbook, *Dimensions of Human Sexuality*, and conducted more than forty workshops on various aspects of the subject. As an undergraduate at the University of Illinois, she spent a year in Cologne, Germany, as a foreign exchange student. She completed her PhD at the University of Oregon in 1982 and was recognized as one of the Outstanding Young Women of America in 1985.

Dr. Miller's interests include the mountains, walking on the beach, and caring for her two miniature dachshunds, Buffie and Schnaupps. She is the folk music director at St. Joseph's Church, where she sings and plays the guitar.

Contents

CHAPTER 1

What Is a Family?

I f someone were to ask you to describe the "typical" American family of the 1990s, what would you say? How would you describe your own family? Is your best friend's family any different from yours? How? Which of the following television programs is a realistic portrayal of today's family: "The Cosby Show," "Roseanne," "My Two Dads," "Doogie Howser, M.D.," "The Hogan Family," "Empty Nest," "The Golden Girls"? As you can see, today's families are characterized by diversity in form and style.

The institution known as the family has undergone numerous fundamental changes since Colonial days. At that time, families were the center of daily life as well as the basic economic and social unit. They focused largely on physical survival rather than emotional closeness. Husband, wife, and children worked together as a team on farms, in family shops, or in businesses. Farming was the predominant way of life for most families, and each member of the family had important responsibilities. Husbands planted and harvested crops while wives supervised help, kept records, tended the garden, and made soap and candles that could be sold. Working at their parents' side, children learned the skills that they would need later in life. As a social unit, the family cared for the sick, the injured, and the elderly. Instruction in reading, writing, and arithmetic was carried out at home, as were religious studies.

THE PATRIARCHAL FAMILY

Historically, the Colonial family was **patriarchal**, meaning that the husband/father was the head of household and was to be respected simply because he was a man. Wealth was determined by how much land and property he owned. Upon the father's death, sons inherited the family's land, property, or business. Sometimes fathers gave land to their children when they reached adulthood or as part of the marriage contract. Weddings were arranged by the parents and considered business deals rather than "love affairs." It was customary for a woman to give all of her property and rights to her new husband as a wedding present, which resulted in her economic dependence upon him.

Think now about your own family. Did your father have a "special" seat at the head of the table? Did you expect your father to work outside the home and support the family? If a promotion in his job meant moving to another place, was it assumed that the family would move? If your mother and father were discussing an issue or a topic and they disagreed on what should be done, did your father have the last word and make the final decision? A yes to any of those questions indicates that some form of patriarchy is still alive in your family.

THE IMPACT OF INDUSTRIALIZATION

During the nineteenth century, radical changes occurred in the family structure because of industrialization. Factories produced labor-saving farm machinery and family necessities. Men migrated to cities to work in factories and earn wages that enabled them to purchase the commodities that were needed by the family. Thus emerged the concept of the man as the "breadwinner" or provider for the family.

The power structure of the family also changed significantly. Children gained power through employment in factories, since they were no longer dependent on their father's land or property for wealth. Women, however, were expected to continue with their responsibilities of running the home and caring for the children. Although many women enjoyed this role, their work in the home brought in no wages. Therefore, men's work outside the home for wages was given higher status than women's work. Based on this working relationship, women continued to be economically dependent upon their husbands.

Thus, industrialization gave birth to our modern concept of the "traditional" nuclear family, with men working outside the home and women staying at home with the children. Were you raised in a two-parent household? If so, did your mother work exclusively at home, or did she also work outside the home? Was power in your family dependent upon who made the most money? Were your parents equal partners in almost everything they did that affected the family? Whom would you identify as the "head of household"? Have you ever asked your mother if she enjoyed her childrearing responsibilities? Have you ever asked your father if he felt a lot of pressure to provide financial support? If you lived in a one-parent household, how did your family function while you were growing up? How was it decided who performed which duties around the home?

The United States has always been referred to as a "melting pot" of people, and the 19th and early 20th centuries brought waves of immigrants seeking a better life for their families. To maintain their culture in this foreign land, they established settlements that kept alive their native language, foods, and celebrations. Non-immigrants often referred to these settlements in slang terms such as "Chinatown" or "little Italy." These immigrants provided cheap labor in the factories, but the entire family had to work for wages in order to survive economically. Women and young children worked twelve- to fourteen-hour days to supplement the family income. How would your life have been different if you had had to work in a factory beginning at age nine or ten? What opportunities would you have missed if you had had to drop out of school in the fourth or fifth grade? How would you have felt if you had been sent to a segregated school based on your national origin? In what ways would your family be different from what it is today?

THE DEPRESSION AND THE WAR YEARS

The years from 1910 to 1960 saw numerous events that challenged the traditional gender-role patterns. During the crisis of World War I, some 25 percent of working-class wives went to work full time outside the home. For the first time, husbands began cooking, doing laundry, and caring for the children to help their working wives. In the Depression years, couples delayed marriage and parenthood and had fewer children than they wanted.

Divorce rates decreased in the 1930s and early 1940s because couples could not afford the $60 needed to pay for a divorce. During World War II, married women were encouraged to work in factories that had defense contracts while their children were in day-care centers. Was it possible that "Woman's place is in the home" was changing? Not yet!

After World War II came the "Baby Boom," and couples married at younger and younger ages. The economy was prospering, and many of the women who worked during the war gave up their jobs and returned to full-time homemaking. Instead of being completely fulfilled through marriage and childrearing as they had expected, these women experienced loneliness and isolation from their husbands. They began to develop close relationships with other women to fulfill their desire for emotional intimacy. Regrettably, husbands felt that financial security was more important than emotional closeness within the family. Therefore, they developed close relationships with other men who had similar business interests.

THE IMAGE OF THE "IDEAL" FAMILY

Have you ever watched the television reruns of "Father Knows Best," "Leave It to Beaver," or "Ozzie and Harriet"? These shows presented an image of the "ideal" family that became the norm for everyone to compare their lives with. The women were happy homemakers who enjoyed cooking, cleaning, and caring for the children while their husbands went happily off to work. The family appeared to be emotionally close and had only minor problems that could be solved within the time of one episode. Husbands were hard-working, but also sensitive and caring, and spent time alone with their wives. As we moved into the tumultuous 1960s and 1970s, however, numerous social movements as well as economic and technological developments changed the structure and life-style of the family even further. The civil rights movement, the feminist movement, the peace movement, and the gay-rights movement all called our attention to various problems within society. Men and women were struggling to be free of unrealistic gender roles and expectations. Because of inflation, the "American dream" of owning a home could often be realized only if both husband and wife worked. Women had careers that raised new questions for married couples, such as, "Who takes care of the children?" The impact of the Vietnam War was far-reaching, and demographers linked the rising divorce rate directly to the war. Divorce in families left women as "heads of household" literally overnight, as the courts usually gave custody of the children to the mother.

THE SEXUAL REVOLUTION

The sexual revolution of the 1970s was another step in the growing acceptance of nonmarital sex when mutual affection and commitment existed in a relationship. Sexual openness was partly the result of the use of the birth control pill, which allowed women to become the sexual equals of their partners. Divorce rates as well as remarriage rates were high, a significant number of unmarried couples were living together, and many pregnant single mothers were keeping their babies and raising them alone. Homosexuals were still a persecuted minority, but they were demanding not only equal rights in jobs, housing, and public accommodations, but parenthood as well.

"The American family" of the 1980s and 1990s differs from the past in numerous ways, but the most important way is simply by definition. Until 1980, the United States Census defined a family as "a group of two persons or more related by birth, marriage, or adoption and residing together." It was apparent, however, that this definition was obsolete and defined a family too narrowly, based solely on biological or legal membership. Therefore, the 1980 Census broadened the definition to include those persons who shared housing and who were involved in emotionally close relationships. Let's look at some of the new "American families" that exist in the 1990s.

Michelle

Although she was only seven years old, Michelle knew that something was different about her family. Almost every night she could hear her parents fighting, and it scared her so much that she had knots in her stomach and lay awake wishing it would end. She couldn't even remember the last time they went on a family outing that didn't end in some kind of argument. Michelle tried to be good and not cause any trouble, but nothing seemed to work. One night when the yelling was extra loud, the neighbors called the police. The next thing she knew, her father stormed out of the house. The quietness was broken only by her mother's crying in bed.

For the next several months, Michelle rarely saw her father. Although she loved and missed him greatly, she didn't miss the fighting. One night her mother told her that they were going to court in a week to meet with a very wise person called a "judge." The judge was going to ask her some questions, and she simply needed to answer honestly and to the best of her ability.

The judge was a nice woman, and Michelle liked her right away. After several easy questions, the judge asked her the most important question, "Whom do you want to live with, your mother or your father?" Michelle loved both of her parents but felt more comfortable with her mother. The judge said that her father would no longer live with them but reassured her that she would still be able to see him. Michelle began to cry uncontrollably, fearing that her father wouldn't love her anymore.

Ramón

Ramón was an orphan who had spent all his life in and out of foster homes. At the age of fifteen, he felt that no one wanted to adopt him, but he had become fairly close to his caseworker, Mrs. Martorano. One afternoon she mentioned that a lawyer named Rick Jansen wanted to meet him. When Ramón asked her why, Mrs. Martorano said that he wanted to adopt a son and she thought they might be a perfect match. Ramon trusted Mrs. Martorano and agreed to a meeting the following day.

It was a sleepless night for Ramón as he wondered what this Mr. Jansen would be like. How old would he be? Mrs. Martorano had said that he was single, but for how long? Would he want a teenager for a son or someone younger? Even if they got along well, would the courts allow a single person to adopt him? Ramón's brain was still racing at 2 a.m., and he finally drifted off to sleep with his headset on. The alarm clock startled him, and he raced into the shower half asleep but full of questions. Mrs. Martorano picked him up promptly, and they drove to the park for their rendezvous. Mr. Jansen was waiting for them. He was much younger than Ramon expected. Rick shook his hand with great strength and assurance and told Mrs. Martorano that he would drop Ramón back at her office at 5 o'clock. With a wink, Mrs. Martorano was in her car and pulled away.

Time flew by faster than Ramón could believe. Rick was down to earth and very sharp. He challenged Ramón to think and asked him questions that no one ever had before. They both laughed as they shot questions at each other. The final question was Rick's. Would Ramon like to spend some more time with him? Without hesitation, Ramón said yes.

Several months passed, and Mrs. Martorano saw Ramón's spirits soar every time she mentioned Rick's name. When she asked whether Rick talked about adopting him, Ramón became withdrawn and sad. Why hadn't Rick said anything one way or the other? She tried to console him, saying that Rick was trying to figure out how to tell him something, but couldn't. She encouraged Ramón to ask Rick why they were spending so much time together. What were his intentions? Even if Rick didn't want to adopt him, maybe they could be friends and spend time together anyway. It would be better to know now whether or not he was going to have a father.

It took Ramón almost all day, but he finally confronted Rick. Rick took a deep breath and said he had always wanted a son and would love to adopt Ramón, but that he had something to tell him first. When the words came out of Rick's mouth, Ramón thought he was kidding. But when he looked into Rick's eyes, Ramón knew he was telling the truth. Rick simply said, "I'm gay!"

Ramón was outraged with Mrs. Martorano, and she simply sat there while he ranted and raved in her office. When he was done, she asked him to think about this person who had so much to offer him and how honest he had been. She asked him if he had been totally honest with Rick. Had he told Rick that he had been arrested once for robbery and once for driving without a license? Rámon hung his head and said no. Mrs. Martorano smiled her "special smile" and said that Rick knew all about his arrest record and it didn't matter to him. Rick had simply said, "If Ramón had had a father who loved him, those things would never have happened." Ramón wondered what it would be like to have a father who cared about him, even if he was gay.

The months dragged by very slowly for Ramón. He couldn't understand what the problem was with his adoption. Rick was a well-respected lawyer and could obviously afford to have a son. Mrs. Martorano tried to reassure him that adoptions involved a lot of paperwork and it would take time for everyone in the system to sign the necessary documents. Was his past arrest record the problem? Maybe his Hispanic heritage had something to do with the delay! What *was* the problem?

After almost a year, Ramón's dream finally came true. Rick Jansen became his legal father. Mrs. Martorano, Ramón's foster parents, and a few of Rick's closest friends had a coming-home party for Ramón. For the first time in his life, Ramón felt as if he really had a place that he could call home. It didn't matter to him that Rick was gay. Was that why his adoption had taken so long and he had had to answer so many questions? All Ramón knew was that Rick was one of the kindest and most loving people he had ever met. Wasn't that the only thing that mattered in a family?

DeeAudra

All her life DeeAudra had known that she wanted to be a mother. Every time she saw a baby in a stroller, her heart ached. She loved taking care of her ten-month-old nephew, Jerome, but it wasn't the same as having her own baby. Besides her mother and grandmother, her seventeen-year-old sister Felicia and Jerome shared the apartment. Although she was only fourteen, Dee knew she was already a better mother than her sister. Felicia just wanted to go out with her friends and have a good time. She never wanted to be bothered with the baby, but she also would not give it up for adoption.

As a freshman at Proviso East high school, Dee had a straight A average and was very popular. She looked much older than she really was, and she began dating a senior named William. After dating for ten months, she knew that she loved him and wanted to have his child. Dee thought he looked extremely handsome in his ROTC uniform and wondered what their baby would look like. Would it have his dimples or her eyes? As graduation approached, William could not decide whether to join the Navy or go to college. Dee loved the way his eyes sparkled and danced as he talked about "seeing the world" and serving his country. But he had also been offered a football scholarship to Notre Dame, and he would be the first person in his family ever to attend college. Dee knew what she would do in his shoes.

The week passed very slowly at school, and Dee couldn't wait for the weekend to share her news with William. When he picked her up and headed for their favorite pizza parlor, she knew that tonight would be perfect. After they had ordered, William said he had wonderful news. She said she too had something to tell him, but that he could go first. William said that he had enlisted in the Navy and was leaving for San Diego in two weeks. The tears welled up in Dee's eyes as she realized that William would never see his baby. But she knew it would be the most beautiful baby in the world, and it would be someone who would love her and need her.

Dwayne

Next Thursday was Dwayne's eighth birthday, and he wondered what his mom would give him, a new Nintendo game or the train set he had been wanting for over a year. He knew that his birthday was very special for his mom, but he wasn't exactly sure what it meant to be conceived through artificial insemination. Who was his father, and where did he live? What kind of person would be a father to a child and never know if it was a boy or girl? Why did Mom talk about her "biological clock running out"? Dwayne never thought of her as old, even though she had turned fifty three months ago. She always told him how much she had wanted a son and that he was her miracle child. He missed having a father and wondered about him frequently, but he enjoyed spending time with his uncles and cousins. They tried to include him on camping, hunting, and fishing trips whenever possible. He persuaded his mom to become a den mother for the Cub Scouts, and he was proud of her ability to work with his friends on their merit badges. But most of all, he treasured the relationship he had with his mom. They could talk about anything. Even when he was in trouble (which seemed like every day), he knew she loved him.

Ken Ho and Eva

For the past eighteen months, Ken Ho and Eva Tau had watched their mother slowly change from vibrant and active to frail and bedridden. Their grandmother explained that their mother had an inoperable tumor and that soon she would die. Therefore, they had to help her as much as possible and share with her all the things that happened every day at school.

Both Ken Ho and Eva wanted things to be as they once were. They were angry that their mother was going to die, and they hated the doctors. Every time she went to the hospital for a treatment, she came home weaker and even more tired. Who was going to take care of them when she died? Could their father grocery shop, cook meals, or do the laundry? How would they get to soccer practice or dance lessons? Would their grandparents live with them permanently, or would they have to spend time alone waiting for their father to get home from work?

The months dragged by, and their mother died in the spring. Grandmother Calcagno left, and Ken Ho and Eva felt isolated and alone. No one understood how they felt now that their mother had died. Even their teachers didn't understand. How were they supposed to do their homework when their father seemed so unhappy? Nothing they did brought a smile to his face anymore. They wished they were dead too!

Ashley

Being a teenager wasn't easy, but being a teenager whose parents were going through a divorce was almost more than Ashley could bear. She and her mother fought all the time—that is, when her mother was talking to her. At times, her mother would ignore her for days. Those were the worst times. At least when they were fighting, her mother was paying attention to her. No matter what she did, it wasn't good enough or right in her mother's opinion. Her hair was too long, her clothes were too wild, and her friends were all supposedly drug addicts! Ashley thought that her mother was the unhappiest and cruelest person in the world. There was no doubt in her mind whom she wanted to live with both during and after the divorce.

Her father was not perfect, but at least they could talk to each other. He had never said a negative word about his wife or hit Ashley. He simply blamed his wife's moody personality on early menopause and said that they were no longer compatible. During the separation, Ashley was told that she would live with each of them for six months and then could decide whom to live with permanently.

Had her father lost his mind? She could never live with her mother for six months without him there to mediate! What was she going to do? Ashley decided to talk to the lawyer and ask him to arrange a family meeting so she could air her feelings in front of both of her parents together. Whose idea was it for her to live with each of them for six months? Had her mother said that she wanted her? No one had asked Ashley what she wanted to do. At fourteen, she thought she was old enough to tell them that she intended to live with her father. No one could make her live with her mother. If they did, she would simply run away and get lost on the streets of Chicago.

The separation and divorce were difficult, but Ashley knew she had made the right decision about living with her father. She and her mother drifted even further apart, and Ashley felt as if her mother didn't even exist any longer. Her pain lessened each day as she became closer to her father. He tried to spend less time at his office and more time with her. They enjoyed going to the movies, bowling, and once in a while horseback riding. She knew he was trying very hard to be both mother and father to her, but Ashley was sixteen now and very independent.

She became active in the young adult group at church and finally persuaded her father to join several of the social functions. It was at a pancake breakfast at church that he met Dorothy.

Dorothy was also a divorcée, and she had two sons, Jason and Eric. They were ten and seven years old respectively and couldn't even remember having a father. Ashley found Dorothy fascinating and easy to talk to. She wondered what it would be like to have a stepmother who could give her advice from a woman's perspective. It was at that instant that Ashley decided to play matchmaker between her father and Dorothy. The only problem was the two boys. How would she feel about having stepbrothers? Would they destroy her relationship with her father, or would she always be "daddy's little girl"?

The pancake breakfast was the first time in a long time that her father had laughed and interacted with other adults in a social setting. They even persuaded him to cook pancakes for an hour and later to wait on tables. From the moment they met, her father and Dorothy seemed like old friends, and Ashley suddenly realized how empty her father's life must be. When was the last time he went out with friends? How many dates had he gone on in the past two years? Three? Four?

After dating for over a year, her father asked Dorothy to marry him. Ashley genuinely cared for Dorothy, but she was apprehensive about having two younger brothers. She enjoyed her special relationship with her father as an only child. Would he prefer having sons over a daughter? Would he no longer need her because of Dorothy?

Adjusting to Jason and Eric was not easy, and Ashley's feelings vacillated daily. One minute she was jealous that her father took the boys hunting or fishing, but a minute later she was relieved that she didn't have to go along.

Ashley knew she would be going away to college in a year and would soon be involved in numerous campus activities. So she was happy to see the way Dorothy looked at her father and to know that he would not be lonely when she left for school. Even though Ashley hated to admit it, it was kind of nice to be able to blame things on her brothers and give them advice. It made her feel needed in a special way! Maybe as they all got older, they would grow closer together as a family.

NEW STYLES OF FAMILIES IN THE 1990s

As you can see, the "American families" of the 1990s are very different. One out of four children is raised by a single parent. Single parenthood results from divorce, adoption, choice, advanced medical technology, or death. In Michelle's case, her parents were divorced and the judge decided that it would be in her best interest if she lived with her mother. As an orphan, Ramón had lived with foster families all his life and had given up hope of ever belonging to a family. Our judicial system has begun to realize that single persons have the same potential as couples to be good parents, regardless of their sexual orientation. Therefore, single men and women have legally become parents through the adoption process.

Adolescent pregnancy is associated with nearly one-fifth of all births annually in the United States. Approximately 93 percent of unmarried adolescent mothers choose to keep the baby, so it is not surprising that DeeAudra will have her baby and raise it by herself. In addition to teenage unwed mothers, single women like Dwayne's mother are choosing parenthood through the use of advanced medical technology. The most common technique is called artificial insemination. In this procedure, semen from a woman's partner, a friend, or an anonymous donor is mechanically introduced into her uterus.

Significant changes have occurred in the last several decades regarding traditional sex-role stereotypes. Men have had to fight for the right to raise their own children, as it was assumed that women inherently possessed better childrearing skills. The death of Ken Ho and Eva's mother has forced Mr. Tau into a role that will be difficult for him, but not impossible. Only time will tell whether or not he has the skills to raise Ken Ho and Eva.

According to a recent article in *Newsweek* (Winter/Spring, 1990), one third of all children born in the past decade will probably live in a stepfamily before they reach the age of eighteen. Ashley lived alone with her father for a couple of years, but she now has a stepmother and stepbrothers. How many of your friends live in blended families?

PREJUDICE TARGETS A NEW GROUP

Despite the fact that all six of the families you just met involved some type of single parent, which child will have the most difficult time growing up in our society? If you guessed Ramón, you were right. There has been considerable controversy over the ability of homosexual parents to provide a positive, healthy family environment for children. This book addresses some of the myths that still surround homosexuality, as well as some of the unique problems that children of homosexual parents may face. Keep in mind, however, that many of these problems are very similar to those faced in heterosexual families. Let's examine what it means to think that your parents (one or both) are homosexual.

CHAPTER ◇ 2

Just Different,
That's All

Have you ever wondered how your parents met or where they went on their first date? Can you imagine them holding hands and strolling through the park? Have you ever invaded your parents' privacy and burst into the bedroom only to be told to "leave immediately"? When was the first time you thought of your parents as sexual beings? Depending upon your age right now, you are probably in the process of discovering who you are, both individually and sexually. At the same time, you are also old enough to suspect that one of your parents is homosexual. You may have had this feeling all your life, or something may have triggered your suspicions recently. If you were really lucky, your parents began at an early age explaining how your family was different from other families. They may even have encouraged you to ask questions whenever you wanted to know something. But in case they didn't, let's define sexual orientation and see what it means if one of your parents is a gay male or a lesbian.

DEFINING SEXUAL ORIENTATION

Our inclination or capacity to develop intimate emotional and sexual relationships with people of the same gender, the other gender, or either gender is called our sexual orientation. Discovering your own sexual orientation, however, may be a slow process that unfolds over many years. It may take until adulthood or even later before you correctly or comfortably identify your sexual orientation. It also took your parents years to determine their sexual orientation. Although sexuality is a component of every human being, sexual orientation may differ considerably.

Before we go any further, we need to define some terms. In the narrowest sense, the term gender corresponds to your biological sex, male or female. Researchers have coined the phrase **gender identity** to refer to your emotional and intellectual awareness of being either male or female. Society often associates specific personality characteristics, attitudes, and behaviors with a particular sex. This is referred to as **gender roles** or **sex roles**. If you were to hear the words "aggressive, dominant, unemotional, competitive," with which sex would you associate those terms? Have you ever wondered why you associate those terms with a male rather than a female? As you can see, trying to describe people and their behavior is not an easy task.

A **homosexual** is someone who develops intimate emotional and sexual relationships with people of the same gender. A **heterosexual** develops relationships with people of the other gender; **bisexuals** become intimately involved with either gender. The words homosexual and heterosexual are derived from Greek roots meaning same and opposite.

Although heterosexuality appears to be the sexual orientation of the majority of people, approximately 10 percent of Americans are openly gay. It is estimated that as many as 25 to 30 percent of the population may be homosexual, but discrimination has forced most gays to keep their life-style a secret. People have very different and strong views on homosexuality. Because of over-emphasis on the sexual aspect of this life-style and the negative feelings that often arise when one hears the word homosexual, most male homosexuals prefer to be called a **gay male** or simply **gay**.

The term **lesbian**, which is used exclusively to refer to female homosexuals, can be traced to the poet Sappho, who lived on the Greek island Lesbos (hence "Lesbian") in the seventh century B.C. She was the head of a school where young women were taught femininity and the erotic arts. Sappho was married and had one daughter, but her passion was writing about her love for other women.

Replacing the term homosexual is critical in expanding our understanding of gay men and lesbians. It enables us to see them as whole persons by emphasizing the fact that sexuality is not the only aspect of their lives: Their lives also include love, commitment, caring, hope, dreams, work, children, politics, religious devotion, and community involvement. Sex is important, obviously, but it is not the only significant aspect of their lives, just as it is not the only significant aspect of the lives of heterosexuals.

Now it's time to meet some of your peers who have lived with the same problems that you are facing. By the time you finish reading this book, you will realize that you are not alone in your concerns, struggles, or "secret." No one can tell you how to respond if you discover that your father is gay or your mother is a lesbian, but perhaps you can gain some insights and direction from the people in this book. See if you already identify with any of their experiences.

Katarina

Sunday was family day, and Katarina looked forward to spending the day with her mom. This Sunday, however, would be extra special, as they were having a party in honor of "Gotcha Day!" Unlike most children who celebrate their birthday once a year, Katarina got to celebrate twice a year: on her birthday and also on the day her mother brought her home from the adoption agency. Her mom always said, "It was the day that I gotcha, and it was the happiest day of my life!" Katarina was now four years old, and she was just beginning to understand what it meant to be adopted. The most important thing to her was that her mom loved her, but she also enjoyed having two parties each year. Katarina knew she was the luckiest little girl in the world.

Sundays were always fun because Regina, her mom's best friend, would play with her all day, have dinner with them, read her a story, and spend the night. Katarina liked that the best because Regina would make break-fast in the morning and walk with them to the day-care center. Katarina loved to walk hand in hand with her two moms and show them all the pictures she had drawn the week before. Tommy was her best friend, and he loved the way Regina swept him off the ground and gave him a giant bear hug. Through the eyes of a four-year-old, life was wonderful and Mondays were a terrific way to start the week.

Shawn

At the age of ten, Shawn knew that his parents weren't happy together, but he couldn't figure out what was wrong. Although both of his parents worked, his mother used to be waiting for him when he returned home from school. He loved the quiet time they shared together then. She always whistled or sang off key to the radio while she made dinner. Now, however, she rarely came home until almost dinner time. He couldn't remember the last time he heard her laugh in the house.

Fifth grade was difficult for Shawn, and his grades were lower than ever before. He received a C- in math and a D in history. His father checked Shawn's homework every night after dinner and would not let him watch television unless it was perfect. Whenever his mother tried to help him, his father said, "Stay away from my son!" What did he mean by "my son"? Wasn't he also her son? Shawn was more confused than ever. He didn't know if he was adopted or if his father had been married before and his mother was not his biological mother. Shawn was afraid to ask his father any questions, so he decided to wait and ask his mother when they were alone together.

Was there a family secret that Shawn did not know about? Who was Tracy, and why did his father refuse to let her into the house? Had she been in jail, or did she sell drugs? Shawn's imagination was running wild, but he knew one thing for sure: He didn't want to continue living in the house the way things were. Something had to change, but he didn't know whether he had the power to fix what was wrong between his parents or if this was what happened when your parents were about to divorce.

Shawn stared at the ceiling and tried to figure out what he should do. Maybe his friend Malcolm could give him some advice during lunch. Shawn tossed and turned all night and ran out of the house without even eating breakfast. He never noticed that his parents were arguing in the dining room, or that his father told his mother to "pack your bags and get out." Shawn also didn't hear the names his father was calling her. But most of all, he didn't see the tears rolling down his mother's cheeks as she spoke in a whisper, "I love you both dearly, but I cannot live this lie any longer."

Elio

The apartment complex that Elio lived in was old and stood on the edge of town near several vacant lots and a junkyard. To Elio, it was a castle surrounded by a moat, and only he could give permission for someone to enter the castle. Elio lived on the top floor with his father and Leonardo. The three of them had lived together for as long as Elio could remember, even if that wasn't very long, as he was only seven years old.

There were lots of children to play with in the building, and Elio liked everyone but Ted. No one really liked Ted; he was a bully and used bad words that got you in trouble with your parents. But Ted was also the best athlete and everyone wanted to win, so they let him play whenever they needed another player to balance the teams.

It was on one such afternoon that Elio first remembers Ted calling his father a faggot. Elio didn't know what it meant, but he could tell from the way Ted said it that it must be bad. The two of them got into a terrible fistfight, and the landlord had to break it up. When Mr. Carson asked them what started the fight, Elio calmly said that Ted had called his father a faggot. Mr. Carson asked if he knew what that meant, and Elio lowered his voice as he said, "No, sir." Mr. Carson said that he should go home and ask his father what it meant.

Later that night, Elio asked his father and Leonardo what "faggot" meant. Both men looked at each other, then at Elio, and his father finally said, "I love you very much, and thank you for defending me today." Elio doesn't remember many of the details of their discussion, but he does remember that his father mentioned the words **homosexual**, **faggot**, and **gay**. When Elio repeated his question, his father simply said that he was called a faggot because he loved Leonardo very much and planned to spend the rest of his life with him. Elio quickly replied, "Then I'm a faggot too, because I love Leonardo very much and I want him to stay with us forever."

Elio never felt comfortable when he heard someone call another person queer, gay, or faggot. It wasn't the words that bothered him so much, but the way people said it and the look in their eyes. He learned quickly that the best thing to do in a crowd was walk away. Otherwise, he always ended up in a fight and had to explain why to his father. He was never afraid of getting hurt, but he saw the tears and pain in his father's eyes and wanted to avoid that if at all possible.

Althea

All during high school, Althea never saw her mom go out on a real date with a man. Her mom had plenty of male friends and went out with a group of people, but she never seemed interested in pursuing a relationship with any one man. Althea, on the other hand, had a steady stream of suitors and dated every Friday and Saturday night. She was active in student council, as well as the French and drama clubs. In addition, she volunteered her time one night a week in a homeless shelter and met lots of interesting people. No one was surprised when her classmates voted her the "most likely to succeed" and "the friendliest female" in the class.

The senior prom was less than two weeks away, and Darryl Bradshaw, the handsomest boy in the class, had invited her to the dance. Althea was going to double-date with her best friend Monique and Monique's boyfriend, William. The excitement was building daily at school, and all the girls talked about were their dresses, dinner, and the beach. The best part of the weekend, though, was spending Saturday night at the beach and sitting around a bonfire with your date. It was tradition for everyone to stay at the beach house and have Mr. and Mrs. McNerny, the guidance counselor and her husband, make pancakes for brunch about noon.

The music at the prom was fantastic, and everyone danced until they were hot, sweaty, exhausted, and hungry. The last set ended at midnight, and Althea, Monique, and their dates headed for dinner at last. On the way to the restaurant, Althea asked Darryl to swing by her house for a minute so she could use the bathroom. As she opened the front door, Althea heard soft music playing in the living room and laughter. No one heard her say, "Hello, anyone home?" She entered the hallway and froze in the shadows of the living room archway. As she gazed in the direction of the laughter and low voices, Althea suddenly knew why her mom never dated any of her male friends. Slow-dancing in the living room were her mom and Jenny.

Althea had always felt there was something special about the relationship between her mom and Jenny, but she could never put her finger on it. Now she knew for sure. Althea tiptoed out of the house very quietly, not wanting her mom to know what she had seen. How could she ever explain to her friends that her mother was a lesbian? Why hadn't her mom ever told her? In the past, they had talked about anything and everything for hours. They didn't always agree, but they respected each other's opinions. Now, however, Althea discovered that she knew very little about her mother's personal life.

As Althea got back into the car, she slid over close to Darryl and he put his arm around her. She began to shake uncontrollably, and her brain raced. What should she do? Should she remain at the beach house or confront her mom with Jenny there? Why was she so upset? Was she angry because she felt deceived, or because her mom seemed so happy with Jenny? Was it any of Althea's business whom her mom dated? Monique always complained that her mother never dated the same man twice, and she was concerned about her contracting AIDS. Jenny, on the other hand, was someone that Althea respected and admired. Was there some rule that said your parents **had** to be heterosexual?

Althea was angry and more confused than ever. Darryl asked her repeatedly what was wrong, and she replied, "Nothing." To cheer her up, he began to kiss her on the neck and tickle her. Althea loved the smell of Darryl's cologne, and soon she began to relax. She decided to stay at the beach house with her friends and enjoy her senior prom. Right now, she wanted to focus all her attention on Darryl. Tomorrow she would try to sort through her feelings about her mom and Jenny.

Koji

The Yaguchis had immigrated to the United States over thirty years earlier, but their Japanese culture was deeply ingrained in the family. Koji lived with his parents, two sisters, and his grandparents in a tiny house in San Diego. They established a Japanese restaurant, and everyone was expected to work long hard hours in the family business. His grandmother greeted the customers at the door, and his younger sisters, ages thirteen and fourteen, cut up food in the kitchen. At times Koji was overwhelmed by his assorted responsibilities. He drove the dilapidated truck to the docks with his grandfather every morning at five. Grandfather Yaguchi selected all his own meats and fish. From the docks, they drove to the farmers' market to select the vegetables for the day. Once at the restaurant, Koji was responsible for unloading the truck, setting and clearing the tables, filling water glasses, and doing dishes. His grandfather supervised the kitchen and cooked many of the daily specials, while his father answered the phone for carry-out orders, handled the cash register, and talked with the customers.

The most fascinating person at the restaurant was Tai, an excellent chef. He was about seven years younger than Koji's father, but he had traveled around the world. Koji could listen to his stories for hours, and Mr. Yaguchi seemed very fond of him, which was unusual in this tightly knit Japanese family. Koji was amazed at the things he overheard his father telling Tai. How could he share such private things with this total stranger? What was the unique bond between these two men?

Grandfather Yaguchi was a soft-spoken, fragile-looking man, but he definitely controlled everything that happened in the family. Koji was shocked one morning to discover that Tai had been fired by his grandfather while his father was at a doctor's appointment. No one would tell him why they had fired Tai. All Koji knew was that the relationship between his father and grandfather was never the same again and that he was forbidden to mention Tai's name. What could his father and Tai have done that was so terrible that his grandfather could not forgive them?

SEXUALITY: MYTHS AND REALITIES

Sexuality is a complex issue consisting of more than sexual pleasure and reproduction. It is a much deeper component of the human personality that begins developing at birth and continues to evolve into old age. The need for love and personal fulfillment is also an important part of sexuality. Healthy sexual and emotional development occurs when you are able to recognize your sexuality as a beautiful, significant part of yourself. Learning to incorporate sexuality into your life responsibly, joyfully, and with integrity is an ongoing process that started long before you can even remember. Your parents also have gone through this very same search for their sexual identity.

Common Myths About Sexual Orientation

Throughout history, certain groups of people have assumed superiority over minority groups. The ancient Romans attempted to eradicate Christians. When the American colonies were first settled, suspected witches were burned at the stake. Women were considered the property of their husbands and denied all legal rights. Under Adolf Hitler, the Nazis asserted the supremacy of the white race, leading to the Jewish holocaust and World

War II. Before the civil rights movement in the United States, the minority group that was persecuted were African Americans. Today, our sex roles are changing very rapidly, and in efforts to adapt, some people developed stereotypical myths to try to explain complex human behavior that is different from their own. Each of the following myths is either totally incorrect or is true for only a small percentage of people. Let's explore the myths together and see if we can discover the truth.

Myth 1: Sexual thoughts, feelings, fantasies, and dreams are abnormal.

Reality: The primary sex organ is not the genitals but the brain. Your brain produces thousands of thoughts a day. Thoughts and feelings are neither positive nor negative, normal or abnormal; they simply exist. The characters, behaviors, and setting may be unacceptable to you in real life, but there are no abnormal thoughts. Is it possible for you to control your thoughts all the time? Would you even want to? Probably not!

Behaviors, however, may be classified as positive or negative, normal or abnormal. Sexual behaviors that are forced, exploitative, unpleasant, or that lower self-esteem are generally categorized as negative behaviors in our society.

No matter how outrageous or detailed our thoughts may be, it does not mean that we want them to come true, that they are going to come true, or that we mean to act them out. Repetitive thoughts that produce anxiety or guilt may be indicative of a deep-seated problem that needs professional help.

Every human being has imagination, some more active than others. As a child, you may have fantasized about rescuing someone from a burning building. Or you may have dreamt that your dog got lost on your family vacation and walked home 100 miles just to be with you. Do you consider those thoughts abnormal; probably not!

The hormonal changes associated with puberty often lead to thoughts, feelings, fantasies, and dreams that have a sexual connotation. These ideas are a healthy part of your imagination and do not indicate a conscious desire on your part to act them out.

Myth 2: If a person has a gay or lesbian experience, he or she is homosexual.

Reality: It is common for adolescents to have crushes or close relationships with peers or older persons of the same gender. Surveys suggest that 10 percent of girls and up to 20 percent of boys have at least one gay experience, which may include adolescent sex "games," mutual masturbation, kissing, caressing, or rubbing against one another. For most teenagers, this period of adolescent experimentation is simply a transient phase.

Myth 3: A person's sexual orientation can easily be identified by his or her appearance and mannerisms.

Reality: Except for a small percentage of cases, it is impossible to tell a person's sexual orientation simply by appearance and mannerisms. The stereotype that all gay males are weak and effeminate is far from the truth. Gay men are found in all walks of life, including such "macho" types as the military, the police, truck drivers, and football players. During the 1960s and '70s, Rock Hudson was a role model for the American boy, and only after his death was it discovered that he was gay. Where were his limp wrists, lisp, and feminine walk?

When you hear the names Walt Whitman and Michelangelo, what is the first thing that pops into your mind? What would the world have missed if these gay males had not given us the beautiful poetry that Whitman wrote or the Sistine Chapel that Michelangelo painted?

Lesbians supposedly dress like men, wear their hair short, and have bold, aggressive personalities. Does this mean that all female doctors, lawyers, teachers, and flight attendants with short hair are lesbians? Would there be a social welfare system today if the lesbian Jane Addams had not had the courage and strength to stand up for what she thought was right? As you can see, heterosexuals and homosexuals share similar fashions, occupations, talents, dreams, concerns, fears, and mannerisms.

Myth 4: Sexual orientation is rigidly fixed from birth.

Reality: Until the end of the 19th century, it was believed that people were either heterosexual or homosexual and there was nothing in between. An early pioneer in sex research, Alfred Kinsey, undertook a monumental study in the 1940s and 1950s that determined that sexual behavior does not fall into two distinct categories, but instead falls somewhere on a continuum. Kinsey's scale on this continuum ran from 0 (exclusively heterosexual behavior) to 6 (exclusively homosexual behavior), with the midpoint of 3 indicating equal amounts of heterosexual and homosexual behavior (bisexuality). This continuum is shown on the next page.

0	1	2	3	4	5	6
Exclusively			Bisexual			Exclusively
Heterosexual						Homosexual

From infancy to old age, everyone goes through normal developmental stages marked by curiosity, sexual experimentation, and contradictory feelings. Whether or not you enjoyed these experiences, made a mistake, or suppressed your feelings, each of these stages gave you an opportunity to grow and become the person that you are today. Your parents have had these same experiences and may have suppressed their sexual feelings for years. Possibly, however, they are now ready to acknowledge who they really are.

Myth 5: The number of gays has increased significantly in the past decade.

Reality: Since the time of Kinsey's report, it has been thought that the United States has experienced a liberating "sexual revolution" that has greatly impacted sexual behaviors. Therefore, almost thirty years later, a journalist named Morton Hunt published *Sexual Behavior in the 1970's.* His book was based on a survey of 982 males and 1,044 females aged eighteen and over. According to his findings, three major changes in sexual behavior have occurred, but none of them indicates an increase in the number of gays in the United States. Instead, Hunt found that premarital intercourse was more common, sex roles were changing, and the differences between social classes were smaller.

Because of the gay liberation movement, gay males and lesbians are increasingly being more open about their sexual orientation with their families and friends and on the job. That does not mean, however, that the number of gays is increasing. It simply means that the gay male or lesbian has learned to lovingly accept himself or herself as "different" and has determined to let go of the secretiveness, fear, and anxiety that he or she has felt.

When Hunt's results are compared to studies done in Sweden and Germany, the results are amazingly similar. Approximately 10 percent of the population publicly identifies themselves as being gay. Thus, the number of gay males and lesbians appears to be relatively stable both over time and across cultures. Have any of your friends ever said that they thought they might be gay? Have you ever questioned your own sexual identity?

Myth 6: People who marry and have children are heterosexual. Homosexual/bisexual people never marry and have children. People who never marry are gay or bisexual.

Reality: Being married and having children is a poor predictor of a person's sexual orientation. True, heterosexuals do marry and have children, but so do many gay males, lesbians, and bisexuals. In fact, it has been estimated that as many as a third of lesbians and a fifth of gay men marry. In addition, approximately 2 to 3 percent of currently married American men engage in extramarital homosexual activity while remaining sexually active with their wives.

Why do people get married? The answer to that question is very simple, but at the same time very complex. Among the reasons people get married: (1) they love their partner; (2) their parents and society expect them to to do so; (3) they want to have children; (4) they seek companionship; and (5) they desire economic security.

Gay males and lesbians marry for all of those reasons, but with a slight twist. First, when two people love each other, it is expected that they will get married. A person can love someone, however, without being sexually attracted to him or her. Also, some gays think they are heterosexual or bisexual, and only later in life become aware of their true sexual orientation.

Second, family expectations and pressures have led many couples to the altar, regardless of sexual orientation. If parents think their son or daughter may be gay, however, they may believe that he or she will "change" after marriage. That is seldom true. You can "change" someone only if the person wants to be changed, and one cannot change sexual orientation as easily as changing shoes. Could you change your sexual orientation if your partner asked you to?

It is not uncommon for one partner to tell the other of a fear of being gay before they are married. The partner really loves this person and convinces him or her that their marriage can erase these doubts. The gay person wants to believe and continues to deny homosexuality. Unfortunately, the gay feelings never go away and the person now tolerates the marriage, but feels "trapped." If your fiancé said he or she thought he or she was gay, how would you respond? Would you believe him or her? Or would you try to "save" him or her?

Third, some gay males and lesbians have always dreamed of having their own biological children and believe that the "conventional" family offers the best environment in which to raise children. Two-parent families have been typical in the past, but with today's soaring divorce rate, single-parent families have become more common. Who is to say that a heterosexual single parent is any more capable and loving than a gay single parent? Our judicial system has slowly recognized that a person's sexual orientation does not determine whether or not one is a fit parent. More and more gay parents who have been divorced are being granted custody of their children. This issue will be discussed further in a later chapter.

According to the psychologist Abraham Maslow, all human beings have five basic needs that must be met in order to achieve emotional well-being. The most primitive needs are related to physical survival—food, clothing, and shelter. After those have been met, a person needs to feel physically safe and secure. Last is the need to be loved and belong to a family or other support group. No matter who you are or what your sexual orientation, you need close relationships with other people.

For heterosexuals, building relationships and choosing a companion follows a logical, socially acceptable path. It starts slowly with a first date, holding hands, and a quick good-night kiss. When they feel comfortable with each other, they begin to relax and more openly show signs of affection, such as an arm around the waist or shoulder or a playful kiss on the cheek. As the relationship continues to grow, the couple may exchange rings or bracelets and announce to family and friends that they are "going steady." Once they are ready for a commitment, they become engaged and the relationship is sealed with a public ritual called a marriage ceremony.

Most new relationships follow a natural progression toward closeness and intimacy. But there is no socially acceptable path for the feelings of a gay couple. Let's look at their predicament. They too start with a first date, hold hands, and exchange a quick good-night kiss. However, the similarity to a heterosexual relationship ends there. What would happen to them if they walked down the street arm in arm? It is illegal for them to marry a person of the same sex, so how do they declare their commitment to each other? How would you feel if you could never touch that "special" person in your life in public?

For some gay males and lesbians, the fear of being harassed for loving someone of the same gender, or the fear of living alone for the rest of their lives is so overwhelming that they choose marriage to someone of the other sex out of desperation and need for companionship. Could you marry someone to whom you were not physically and emotionally attracted?

In 1990, according to the U.S. Bureau of Labor Statistics, 65 percent of women over sixteen were employed or looking for work. If so many women were employed or looking for work, why would a lesbian marry to become economically secure? Did your grandmother work outside the home? Does your mother currently work outside the home?

Even though more and more women are working, most of them earn low wages at "pink-collar" jobs rather than having high-paying professions. Title VII of the 1964 Civil Rights Act prohibited discrimination in pay and employment, but it did not end the salary differences between men and women. Occupational segregation by sex is as widespread today as it was at the turn of the century. For example, very few of the engineering graduates from our nation's colleges and universities each year are women. Think back to when you were in elementary school. How many male teachers did you have? Salaries in traditional male occupations (corporate executive, professional athlete, construction worker) are often twice as much as those found in traditional female occupations (nurse, secretary, teacher). Statistically, women earn 69 percent of what men earn. Considering the disparity in both status and pay between most men's and women's occupations, is there any doubt that some women marry solely for economic security?

Myth 7: Historically, heterosexuality has been the only accepted sexual orientation.

Reality: Archeological expeditions have uncovered countless descriptions and references to gay and bisexual lifestyles. According to some sources, one of the oldest records of homosexual love is depicted on an Egyptian papyrus thought to be more than 4,500 years old.

Through the writings of Aristotle, Socrates, Sophocles, and Euripedes (Greek philosophers, a playwright, and a dramatist who were all gay), we know that the Cretans were the first Greeks who regulated their population by encouraging gay male relationships with adolescent boys. It is important, however, to understand the Greek culture. Men were the focus of all intellectual life, and women simply handled household matters and bore children. It was customary for every man to tutor an attractive male youth and bring him as near as possible to the "ideal" of an excellent citizen. This meant that the older man acted as his counselor, guardian, and friend and taught him all the manly virtues. They were together from early morning to late evening every day.

The Greek ideal of male perfection emphasized beauty in both body and soul. Therefore, Greek boys spent three quarters of the day in the gymnasium developing their bodies. The male body was so highly prized that all youths were naked during these exercises. Throughout Greek literature, homosexual love was always idealized and admired and mythicized.

Many of the Greek mythological heroes have been linked to gay behavior. Famous pairs in Greek literature include Zeus and Ganymede, Apollo and Hyacinthus, Pan and Daphnis, and Achilles and Dionysius.

It is a striking fact of history that some of the greatest rulers, scientists, poets, authors, and philosophers have had gay or bisexual orientations. But all of these historical figures are remembered for what they did or did not accomplish, not for their sexual orientation. Do you recognize the following names?

Julius Caesar and Nero, Roman Emperors
Richard the Lion-Hearted, King of England
Peter the Great, Tsar of Russia
Leonardo da Vinci, Florentine scientist and painter
Louis XIII, King of France
Sixtus IV, Italian Pope
Henry David Thoreau, U.S. poet and author
Oscar Wilde, British playwright
Hans Christian Andersen, Danish author of fairy tales
Dag Hammarskjöld, Swedish Secretary-General of the United Nations

Myth 8: Professionals (psychiatrists, psychologists, ministers, etc.) can change your sexual orientation.

Reality: In recent times, the public attitude toward homosexuality has shifted from the belief that gay males and lesbians are sinners to the belief that they are mentally ill. Drastic measures have been used by the medical and psychological professions to "cure" gay males and lesbians. During the 1800s gay males were castrated (surgical removal of the testes). As medical technology advanced, lobotomies were performed (surgery that severs nerve fibers in the frontal lobe of the brain). Since both of these "cures" were unsuccessful, doctors experimented with drugs, hormones, hypnosis, shock treatment, and psychotherapy, all to no avail. For most of the 20th century, the field of psychiatry classified homosexuality as a sexual deviation in its official *Diagnostic and Statistical Manual of Mental Disorders (DSM)*. Research on homosexuality was scant because people were afraid to admit their sexual orientation. Therefore, scientists could study only gays in prison populations or those undergoing psychoanalysis. Consequently, the data indicated that gays were emotionally disturbed and in need of professional help.

In 1973 the *DSM-III* of the American Psychiatric Association (APA) came up for revision. After conflicting evidence had been presented to the chairman of the APA Task Force, he ruled that a "significant portion of gay males and lesbians" were satisfied with their sexual orientation, showed no significant signs of mental illness, and could function well interpersonally, socially, and vocationally. As a consequence, homosexuality was deleted from the list of mental disorders in the revised DSM-III.

Up to that time, anyone who was not heterosexual was considered to be "abnormal" and sick. Following that line of thinking, then, professionals should be able to "cure" you if you are "different" from the majority. Let's look at an example and see if that logic is valid.

Todd has just moved into town from Texas and has entered the ninth grade at East Leyden High School. Mr. Redman introduces Todd to the class and assigns him a seat across from yours. There's nothing unusual about Todd as he slides into his seat, and you mumble a quick hello. As Mr. Redman continues the algebra lesson, you begin to observe Todd carefully. Suddenly, something catches your eye. Without even realizing it, you jump up and tell the class to look at Todd. Bewildered, Todd asks what is wrong. In unison, the class shouts: "You are left-handed."

Psychiatrists, psychologists, and other professionals are only capable of helping troubled and dissatisfied people, regardless of their orientation. Once your sexual orientation has been determined, it is not something that can be changed like a pair of socks; it is a permanent part of you like your race. How would you feel if you were Todd and the school sent you to a professional to "cure" your left-handedness?

Myth 9: Gay males are child molesters.

Reality: Current statistics from police departments and child protective agencies across the nation show that the overwhelming majority of child molestations (80 to 97 percent) involve adult heterosexual males and young females. In fact, a very small proportion of child molestations are attributed to gay males. This myth is part of what some psychologists have called **homophobia**, fear, hatred, or intolerance of gay males, lesbians, bisexuals, or cross-gender behavior. It also includes a pervading fear that gays are continually looking for potential involvements and capitalize on the vulnerability of youth. Nothing is further from the truth. In fact, most child molestation is committed by family friends, relatives, or acquaintances, not gays.

Fear of being identified or labeled gay prevents many people from expressing feelings and emotions that seem natural and normal, especially if they involve physical contact. It takes tremendous courage in today's society to be different and acknowledge those differences openly. The next chapter deals with the struggle that a parent faces in trying to tell his son or daughter that their family is different from others in a unique way. Think about how you would tell your children that you were gay. Would you know how or where to begin? Probably not! Let's see how the parents in the next chapter handle the situation.

CHAPTER 3

Reconciling Dual
Identities

As painful as it is for any child to suspect or learn that one or both parents are gay, it is equally agonizing for parents to decide whether, when, and how to tell their children. Many factors enter into making this decision wisely: the age of the child, the stability of the relationship, and most important, the level of trust that exists between parent and child.

The question of whether or not to tell the child is the biggest obstacle. Is it better to be open and honest, or is it wiser never to acknowledge the relationship for what it is? Can a child raised in an atmosphere of love and support in a homosexual environment deal with the roller coaster of life as effectively as a child raised in a heterosexual environment?

Every gay parent must make this decision based on the strength of the family structure. Does it put more pressure on a child to know of and defend an alternate life-style, or does the truth provide a stronger base from which to grow? There is no one right answer, but according to André Gide, "It is better to be hated for what one is than loved for what one is not."

Once the decision is made to tell the child, the question then becomes how to do so. A parent needs to realize that there are many reactions to this self-disclosure. Shock, disbelief, anger, uneasiness, rejection, and support might be some of the expected reactions. The parent must be ready to deal with the consequences.

A survey of the literature and interviews with children of gay parents address these questions and concerns. This chapter may make you more empathetic to your parent's predicament. At the very least, you'll understand that one or both of your parents thought long and hard before telling you the truth. Would you have been so truthful if you were telling them that *you* were gay?

RESEARCH ON CHILDREN OF GAYS

In 1987, more than 1.5 million gay or lesbian couples were living together. According to the U.S. Bureau of the Census, 92,000 of these couples had children living with them. As you can see, there are a lot of children with this "secret," and you are not alone if you suspect one of your parents is gay. But what is the impact of your gay parents' life-style on you? You are the only one who can answer that question specifically, but the results of numerous studies are not surprising. More than thirty-five studies in the past fifteen years have shown that children of gay parents are no more likely to become gay and are just as well adjusted as other children.

Unlike the common cold, measles, mumps, or chicken pox, no one to date has "caught" homosexuality. If you really believe that one could "catch" sexual orientation, how would you explain children raised in single-parent families who are heterosexual? Or what about children raised by heterosexual parents who are gay? Homosexuality is **not** transmitted from parent to child, nor is it transmitted from gay parent to child. It is still estimated by researchers that one in four parents will have a gay child. Who knows, **you** may be the parent of a gay child some day.

Jean-Claude

The leaves had fallen off the trees months ago, and Jean-Claude could see his breath as he walked to school. Old Man Winter was right around the corner, and it brought back haunting memories. Jean-Claude was skiing with his father when a freak avalanche swept them off the side of the mountain. One minute they were skiing side by side, and the next minute his father had vanished in a cloud of snow. The body was recovered two days later, but Jean-Claude was rescued within five hours. During those five hours, he prayed and wondered who would take care of his mother if both of them died.

The accident had happened six years ago, but it was still vivid in his mind. Even though his uncle lived less than two miles away, he missed his father. Jean-Claude knew his father would understand when he said he "preferred boys to girls." His mother never talked about his sexual orientation, but she made him read every article about AIDS that she could find. He often wondered why he was gay, but it didn't really matter to him anymore. Jean-Claude just knew that he was a warm, caring person and that God had spared his life. To Jean-Claude, that was a sign that he had the strength to deal with the persecution he experienced daily as a gay male. If only his mother could overcome her anger at having a gay son!

Rebecca Jo

"My dad was a gay male before I was born. He and my mom were never married because she is a lesbian. I have been around gay people all my life, and they have treated me with respect and dignity. I don't remember my first gay march in Washington, D.C. because I was only three months old.

"I have always lived with my dad and have no regrets about my childhood. He and Mohammed have been lovers for almost fourteen years, and I love the way the two of them spoil me. The funniest part about growing up in an all-male household is that all of us had to learn 'girl things' together. In the fourth grade, the school nurse taught us about the menstrual cycle. I was shy and didn't ask any questions. The look on my father's face was priceless when I asked him to take me to the drugstore to buy sanitary pads. Neither Mohammed nor my father knew how to braid my hair or purchase a bra, but we all learned together.

"Most of my friends were allowed to date at the age of fifteen, but my fathers thought sixteen was soon enough. I was not allowed to go out on week nights unless it was a school function like a basketball game or a concert. My curfew was 11 p.m., and they both waited up for me after a date. Each date started with twenty questions: Where were we going? With whom? Who was driving? Would alcohol or drugs be at the party? Were the parents going to be home? Although I hated all the questions, I felt that they loved me wholeheartedly. I knew I could call either one of them at any time and be picked up and brought home safely without a lot of questions.

"Did I think they were too strict and overprotective? Probably, but I had two parents who wanted me to be happy, and they both looked forward to being grandfathers some day. And I knew that some day I would be a wonderful wife and mother. I only hoped that I would marry a man just like 'my two dads.'"

Being gay is not something that you "catch" or inherit from your parents. If your father has freckles, it doesn't mean that you will too. If your mother has a birthmark on her neck, it doesn't mean that you will have one also. Jean-Claude and Rebecca Jo are no more likely to be maladjusted than any other child. Your sexual identity will unfold over time, and it is hoped you will accept it with open arms.

The children of gay parents are like all young people. Those whose parents love them unconditionally, spend quality time with them, encourage autonomy, and help them develop critical thinking skills and problem-solving skills develop a positive self-concept, and a close relationship with their gay parent. These are the attributes that every parent wants his or her child to develop in today's world. Children who do not develop these qualities have a hard time surviving in the competitive nature of the American society.

While many gay males and lesbians cherish their roles as parents, not everyone makes a good parent. Let's see what happens to Anastasia.

Anastasia

The transition from a public middle school to a private high school was very difficult for Anastasia. She hated the blue plaid skirt, white blouse, and loafers that comprised her uniform. The boys were mostly nerds, and the athletic teams consistently finished at the bottom of the conference. Anastasia felt lost at this new school and wished she had died over the summer rather than enroll here. Nazareth Academy had a progressive curriculum, computers in the library, several foreign languages, and a small teacher/pupil ratio. Her largest class had eighteen students. Anastasia was very bright, but she had no desire to go to school or learn anything that her teachers taught.

Anastasia fought with her mother all the time; that is, whenever she was home. Her mother worked two jobs, one as a paralegal and the other in a feminist bookstore from eight to midnight six nights a week. Only a few of Anastasia's closest friends knew that her mother was a lesbian. Anastasia enjoyed the freedom that her mother's schedule afforded her. She hung out at the corner drugstore with a group of upperclassmen and dated Otto, who had his own car. She cut school so often that she almost failed the eighth grade. If she hadn't been caught drinking in the bathroom so many times, Anastasia would be attending the public high school with her friends. However, her mother's lawyer made a deal with the school district that if they promoted Anastasia she would not attend the public high school for at least two years, or until she went through a drug rehabilitation program and met with a therapist. Anastasia knew that her mother just wanted her to graduate and didn't care if she went to the drug rehabilitation program or not. According to her mother, therapists were a waste of time and money. So

Anastasia continued dating Otto and stealing alcohol out of her mother's liquor cabinet.

Anastasia doesn't remember much about her freshman year at Nazareth Academy, but she knew she loved Otto. He showed her how much he loved her when he shared his crack with her. They made love while she was high, and it was a night she will never forget. Five weeks later she discovered that she was pregnant and Otto had a new girlfriend.

For years people have been asking, "Which came first, the chicken or the egg?" In Anastasia's story, we have a similar question, but the answer is much easier. Did the lesbianism of Anastasia's mother cause Anastasia's truancy, drug addiction, and promiscuity, or was her mother a lousy parent? You could probably debate that question with your friends, but Anastasia's mother was simply a lousy parent. She did not spend any time with her daughter, and she took no interest in Anastasia's health and well-being. Not everyone possesses parenting skills. Quality parenting takes a lot of hard work, unconditional love, time, patience, and desire. If these ingredients are missing in either of your parents, it will be very difficult for you to develop a close relationship with him or her.

THE MISSING PIECE

Divorce is one of the most important forces affecting and changing American lives today. The divorce rate began to skyrocket in the mid-1960s and has just recently leveled off. Researchers in 1974 reported for the first time in history that more marriages ended in divorce than by death. Today, between 50 and 60 percent of all new marriages are likely to end in divorce. Think about your closest friends. How many of them have divorced parents? Are your parents divorced? Or are they in the process of becoming divorced?

Who is responsible when a couple decide to divorce? If no children are involved, everyone would acknowledge the couple as being responsible for the separation. But when children are involved, the children often feel responsible for the disintegration of the family structure. Although children respond differently to divorce at various ages, numerous research studies indicate that children often think their behavior, temperament, or gender may have caused the breakup of their family.

After months or years of feeling responsible for your parents' divorce, you may be relieved to discover what went wrong with their marriage. You may have been carrying around an enormous amount of guilt for your parents' divorce, and the pressure is finally off you when your parent acknowledges his or her gay identity.

Although your parents may not have told you the reason or reasons for their divorce, it is possible that they separated because one of them was gay and decided it was time to acknowledge his or her sexual orientation. Therefore, you may be dealing with a variety of interwoven issues. Not only are you adjusting to the divorce, but also to a new family structure and the revelation of a parent's sexual orientation. Which is more disruptive to you, your parents' divorce, or the discovery that one of your parents is gay? Take a few minutes to think about that question.

TO TELL OR NOT TO TELL, THAT IS THE QUESTION

The author George Bernard Shaw said in a speech, "When you prevent me from doing anything I want to do, that is persecution; but when I prevent you from doing anything you want to do, that is law, order, and morals." If you think about that statement, you can understand why so many gay males and lesbians never publicly acknowledge their sexual identity. To avoid discrimination in their families, jobs, housing, religion, and friendships, they remain "closeted" or "invisible"—hidden to those around them. The 1964 Civil Rights Act prohibits discrimination based on sex, color, race, national origin, or religion, but a person's sexual or affectional preference is not protected by this legislation. How would you feel if you were Jay?

Jay

All his life Jay had known that he wanted to be a chef. He spent hours watching his grandmother, father, and older sisters cook. His first job in high school was as a busboy in Antoine's, one of the nicest restaurants in New York. Every chance he got, he asked questions of the master chefs and begged to taste whatever they were preparing. He could barely think about his classes at school and waited eagerly for the final bell so he could go to the restaurant.

After graduation from high school, Jay began to work full time at the restaurant. Although his questions became tiresome for the chefs, they knew that one day he would ask them about the various culinary schools in the United States and Europe. Jay began working on an associate degree in restaurant management at a technical college, but his passion was cooking. He loved to host parties for his family and friends and soon was hired by a catering service to work weddings and special events.

By age twenty-five Jay had completed his degree, worked in four major restaurants, and knew it was time to advance his culinary skills. He surveyed all of the head chefs and narrowed his choices down to the following schools: Johnson and Wales University at Charleston, South Carolina, the Culinary Institute of America in Hyde Park, New York, or the American Culinary Federation Educational Institute in Chicago, Illinois. He decided it was time to leave the New York area, and he selected Johnson and Wales. He completed its program as the number one graduate and was accepted as an apprentice with François Delorose, Atlanta's acknowledged chef. After three years in Atlanta, he attended Leith's School of Food and Wine in London and the École Lenotre pastry school in Paris. Jay's passion for cooking grew with every accomplishment, and he returned to New York to be closer to his family.

Sorting through the numerous job offers was difficult, but Jay settled on Dominique's in the Alexander Hotel. The restaurant offered traditional elegance and a few exotic items. He knew he could create masterpieces in the kitchen that his patrons would enjoy. The restaurant critics loved the new dishes that Jay added to the menu, and for the first time in his life Jay felt like a whole person. He was thrilled with his job, and he had just celebrated his five-year anniversary with Ricardo. Life was wonderful!

Because of Ricardo's occupation as a pilot for United Airlines, Jay and Ricardo had to make the most of their time together. Ricardo's schedule changed frequently, but

Jay could fly anywhere with him provided there was an empty seat on the plane. It was after a three-day weekend in Denver that Jay returned to work to discover that he had been fired and replaced by another chef. The mâitre d'hotel's only comment was, "What would the patrons think if they knew that the man preparing their food was gay?"

No one at Dominique's questioned Jay's culinary skills. He had studied in world-renowned institutions and apprenticed under master chefs. But Jay's gay life-style was used to discriminate against him. How would you feel if this master chef prepared food for you? If you think you would be uncomfortable, you might want to examine your own feelings about homosexuality. How would you feel if you had studied for years to become a master chef and then were fired for your sexual orientation?

The process of publicly acknowledging one's gayness is referred to as "coming out" or "coming out of the closet." This is a courageous step for anyone, but especially for a gay parent. Your gay parent wants you to know who he or she really is, rather than some false persona. It has probably taken years for him or her to internalize and acknowledge a gay identity. To maintain integrity as a parent, self-disclosure seems the only answer. Analyze how you feel after reading Carole's story.

Carole

"All my life I have known that I wanted to parent a child. For the majority of women, this is an assumed choice. However, I fall into a category of people for whom the choice takes a different twist. I am a lesbian who has lived in a monogamous relationship with a very special person for the last ten years and will live the rest of my life with her.

"Like any other couple, we would love to have children. But why did I want to have a child? It was very hard not to look at this desire from a selfish standpoint. Was I placing a child in a life of turmoil and confusion simply to meet a need of my own? Or could the two of us offer a child a life of love and fulfillment that he or she might not have otherwise? My partner and I spent hours, days, and literally years contemplating and discussing the pros and cons of the situation. It is hard to imagine any parents doing more soul-searching over whether to have a child.

"With a firm belief that I was doing the right thing, I sought the help of a lawyer to begin the adoption process. After more than two and a half years of intense evaluation, we were blessed with the adoption of a one-year-old girl. The true test of loving and nurturing came at age five when we faced the task of attempting to tell this precious child that she lived in a home environment that many considered unnatural or even deviant.

"What could we possibly say to prepare her for the world's assault on homosexuals? To the best of our ability, we explained to her that some people accepted only the traditional male and female parental role models. What was important to us, however, was being able to model for a child such things as love, trust, expression of feelings, and respect.

"A five-year-old can appreciate truth, honesty, and support for all it is worth. Although we know we face many difficult times ahead, we have to the best of our ability laid a firm foundation that we believe will withstand the prejudice of our society."

*   *   *

Many gays take an active part in parenting their children, and this usually involves frequent contact, especially if you are not living with him or her. The more time you spend with your gay parent, the greater the likelihood you will discover on your own that your parent is gay. Rather than waiting for this discovery, gay parents generally believe that it is better and easier simply to tell their children as soon as possible.

In addition, how would you feel if your gay parent introduced you to his or her new partner and you didn't even know your parent was gay? Would you feel betrayed or angry? Would you have been supportive of their relationship if you had had time to think about it and adjust? No one would benefit from such a situation, and it may cause irreparable damage to the gay parent/child relationship. Therefore, many gay parents feel that it is imperative to tell their children early about their gay identity.

Dave and Jim

Consider the situation that faced Dave and Jim's mom. At the time of their parents' divorce, the boys were thirteen and fifteen years old, respectively. Mike, the father, was awarded custody, and the children lived with him until he decided to remarry and move away from Chicago. Not wanting to leave their friends, school, and other family members, the boys, now fifteen and seventeen, asked to live with their mother.

Julia was thrilled with their request but also faced a dilemma of sorts. Since the breakup of her marriage, she had become involved with another woman. Julia had known Rhonda for years. They worked together for ten years and frequently got together socially. There had always been a sense of connection between them, and the boys were used to seeing Rhonda around the house. At this point, Julia was living with Rhonda in what she considered a long-term committed relationship.

How should Julia approach her sons with this news? Should she let them move in first and gradually become comfortable with the relationship, or should she try to explain it ahead of time? Believing the boys were old enough to handle the truth, she chose to tell them ahead of time. The decision continued the pattern of openness and honesty that had always existed in her relationship with the boys.

In your opinion, did Julia make the right decision? Would you have gone to live with Julia if you were Dave or Jim? Why or why not? How would you feel if you were Rhonda and suddenly had two male teenagers in the house? Would you try to coparent the boys, or would you try to become their "friend"? If you were Rhonda, would you ask Julia to choose whom she wanted to live with, you or her sons? What would have happened to Julia's relationship with her sons if she had simply said, "Your father has custody and you may not live with me now"? Was it fair for Dave and Jim to put their mom in this position?

None of these questions have easy answers, but notice how many people's lives are affected by each decision. Julia loves her sons deeply and wants to continue parenting them, but it may cost her the relationship with Rhonda. Not knowing about their mother's dual identity (she knows she is a lesbian but the boys think she is not), Dave and Jim have no idea the turmoil that their simple request has caused. Meanwhile, the boys' father has remarried and is starting a new life for himself. Where will Dave and Jim fit into that family?

All of the previous examples have resulted in a decision by the gay parent to be honest with the child about his or her sexual orientation. Sometimes, parents decide that it may do more harm than good in their relationship, and they choose to keep their sexual identity hidden. In the following situation, Ken decided **not** to disclose. Let's examine his decision and see what reactions we have to keeping the family "secret."

Lynda

Lynda's parents have been divorced for several years and she has been living with her mother. In July she learned that her mom was going to be transferred to another school district and they would need to move. As a very involved high school student, Lynda began to discuss the possibility of living with her dad. This would allow her to finish her last year of high school with her friends and also to fulfill her many school obligations. She was president of the senior class, played on the volleyball and tennis teams, and was a member of the debate team. To obtain the numerous college scholarships that she was trying so hard to win, it was important for Lynda to remain at her old school.

Lynda's relationship with her father is great, and they frequently spend time together. Since both parents are teachers, Lynda could understand her dad's financial need to rent part of his three-bedroom home to a friend. Barry, Ken's housemate, was a counselor at the Mental Retardation Center. He seemed to be a bright, caring, expressive person. Overall, Lynda's impression of him was definitely positive. She thought she could be very comfortable living with her dad and Barry, and since there were three bedrooms, moving in with them should cause little disruption in their lives.

At first, Ken was very apprehensive about the move. He had never told his daughter that he was gay, and he wasn't certain that a nine-month stay necessitated this self-disclosure. The last thing he wanted to do was jeopardize their relationship. After many long conversations with Barry, he decided not to share his "secret" with her. He and Barry were willing to be discreet enough to not let their relationship become an issue. They were convinced that it was not in Lynda's best interest to be told.

What is your reaction to Ken's decision? Would you feel betrayed if you found out that your father was gay from someone other than him? Would being told or finding out change your feelings about your dad? How difficult was this situation on Barry? How much respect does Ken have for his daughter? How would you feel if you were unable to express your love for your partner in your own home? Could you abstain from any overt signs of affection for over nine months?

THE BEST-LAID PLAN GONE AWRY

In any relationship, the attitude and support of each partner greatly influences the decision-making process. When facing the issue of disclosure, the strength of the bond has a tremendous effect on the choice. The easiest and smoothest transition occurs when the gay and nongay parent can separate with a sense of trust and respect and with your best interest at heart.

If the nongay parent is uncomfortable or defensive about the sexual orientation of the ex-spouse, a tug-of-war may take place over you. The nongay parent may try to alienate you from the gay parent or make you as uncomfortable with the situation as he or she is. It is in this setting that the relationship between you and your gay parent's partner becomes important. Under favorable circumstances, you may have had the opportunity to spend time with this person and to form an opinion of him or her as a person first—without a label. If you have had a chance to observe this person in an atmosphere of love and caring, the groundwork of transition has a firm base on which to rest. However, if you initially meet this person after having been told of the relationship, resentment and confusion may occur. Or, if the nongay parent chooses to disclose the news in a negative manner in an effort to polarize you, the chances of acceptance and understanding are greatly reduced.

Although a great amount of thought should go into the decision to tell a child about one's homosexuality, it is obvious that timing is of critical importance. The best-intentioned parent may have the choice of appropriate disclosure taken away by a resentful spouse.

"WE HAVE A DREAM"

The gay parents interviewed had one resounding thought that they wanted to leave with you in this chapter. It is not easy telling a child that you are a gay male or a lesbian. But they want children to develop a positive sensitivity to gays and to others who are discriminated against. Only then can all people who are persecuted become "visible" to the world and embrace their own self-identity. Is this too much for a parent to ask?

CHAPTER ◇ 4

Living with a Secret

G ay parents and children live in a world that does not accept homosexuality and frowns even more upon gay parenting. For many people, homosexuality and parenting are mutually exclusive terms. Florida and New Hampshire still prohibit gay males and lesbians from adopting children. It has taken over two decades of research showing that children in gay homes were just as well adjusted as children in nongay homes for our legal system to change. The sexual orientation of a parent was often the deciding factor in custody suits, and only recently have legal precedents been established to overcome this obstacle for gay parents. However, judges still retain enormous discretionary powers to determine the suitability of an individual for parenting. Depending on the biases of the family court judge, therefore, it is still entirely possible for the judge to rule that a gay male and a lesbian are unfit parents. Let's eavesdrop on Judge Rivers's courtroom and see if he is consistent in his rulings, or if his prejudices get in the way of the best interest of the child.

Judge Rivers

Mai-Ling was frightened in the large courtroom and couldn't understand what was happening. It was hard for a four-year-old to see snarling faces, her mother crying, and the pain on her father's face. They had been in and out of this very same courtroom at least half a dozen times in the last year. What is a lawyer? Why does Mai-Ling's mother need a lawyer to talk to Judge Rivers? Mai-Ling had met with Judge Rivers in his chambers and found him to be very nice; he even let her select a lollipop from a candy jar on his desk. Why did everyone keep asking her whom she wanted to live with? She wanted to live with her mother and father. It had been very hard adjusting to seeing her father only on weekends. But she loved all the places he took her, and he never went to the office on weekends like he used to. Mai-Ling basked in the attention that her father showered upon her, but she wanted their family to go back to how they used to live— together.

Her father's lawyer, Mr. Goldberg, began to speak, but Mai-Ling heard only part of what he said. Mr. Goldberg said that her father had "fallen off the wagon" because of the stress of the separation, but that he had joined Alcoholics Anonymous. Mai-Ling was astonished; she never even knew that her father owned a wagon! Maybe he would pull her in it next weekend.

After more than an hour, Judge Rivers said that it was time for lunch. He said that at two o'clock he would make a decision. Mai-Ling was surprised that it would take such a wise man so long to decide what he wanted for lunch. She knew she wanted a chili dog with cheese and onions.

They returned to the courtroom shortly before two, and the tension was unbearable. Her father winked at her, and she waved back at him. She was trying to be brave, but she began to tremble as Judge Rivers walked back into the courtroom. Mai-Ling's mother held her hand as he began to speak. "After my interview with Mai-Ling and carefully reviewing the transcript, I rule in favor of Mrs. Woo. There shall be joint legal custody of the minor child Mai-Ling. If Mr. Woo continues with AA and remains sober for at least six months, he may keep Mai-Ling one weekend out of the month and see her every other weekend. Mr. Woo must report back to this courtroom in six months with proof of sobriety before he may share in decisions about Mai-Ling's education, religious training, and general upbringing."

Her mother hugged her so hard that she could barely breathe. As she turned around, she saw another little girl about her own age also waiting for Judge Rivers. Mai-Ling walked over and introduced herself. "My name is Mai-Ling, what's yours?" The girl dropped her eyes and simply said, "Thuy." Mai-Ling squeezed Thuy's hand and said that everything would be okay. Plus, she could pick any flavor lollipop she wanted.

Thuy

The courtroom setting was just as intimidating to four-year-old Thuy as it was to Mai-Ling. Her parents had been separated for eighteen months, and they fought worse than ever when they were together. Thuy wanted to run away and have Ingrid hold her and stroke her hair. That always made Thuy feel safe and relaxed. Ingrid was her mother's best friend, and she lived with them. The three of them had a wonderful time together, but she missed her father. She didn't miss his drinking or violent outbursts, but she missed wrestling with him on the living room floor after dinner. Mr. Pham also took her to the Atlanta Braves baseball games, and he even caught a foul ball for her once. She still displayed it proudly on the bookcase beside her bed.

Before they entered the courtroom, Thuy's mother told her that the most important thing for her to do was tell the truth. Thuy never lied, and she wondered why her mother looked so sad today. Mr. Baker, Mrs. Pham's lawyer, and Mr. Southwick, Mr. Pham's lawyer, talked with the judge in hushed voices. Judge Rivers then took Thuy to his chambers for a discussion of his own.

Judge Rivers appeared to be a powerful man, but he didn't get violent the way her father did. He began to ask her questions, and at first they were very easy to answer. "What's your favorite activity in preschool?" Drawing. "Do you go to church on Sundays with your mother?" Yes, the three of us go every Sunday, and I go to Sunday school with the other children. "Do you have your own bedroom?" Yes, and I have a canopy bed. "Does your mother have her own bedroom?" No, we have a tiny apartment, and my mother and Ingrid share a bedroom. "Who is Ingrid?" Mother 2. "Whom do you want to live with?" I want to live with my mother and father, but . . . Judge Rivers didn't listen to the rest of her answer. He simply offered her a lollipop and said he would fix everything.

Thuy left the judge's chambers and skipped down the hall happily. She couldn't wait to tell her mother that the judge was going to fix everything. Mr. Pham would stop his drinking and violent outbursts, and they could move back into the large house they once lived in. Ingrid could have her own bedroom, and she wouldn't have to share her car with Thuy's mother any longer. Thuy was excited, but she didn't mind sitting quietly in the courtroom for a little while longer, because soon they would be one happy family again.

A police officer and Judge Rivers finally entered the courtroom. "After my interview with Thuy and carefully reviewing all the evidence, I find in favor of Mr. Pham. He shall have sole custody of the minor child Thuy. Mrs. Pham may keep the child one weekend out of the month and see her every other weekend, provided she terminates her lesbian life-style. If she continues her lesbian life-style, all visitation rights are revoked. This court is dismissed."

Before she even knew what was happening, the police officer was restraining her mother and her father swooped her into his arms and out of the courtroom. Thuy was kicking and screaming, "I want my mother," as they drove away in a taxicab.

Go back through both of these hearings and note the similarities between the characters. Why did Judge Rivers rule that Mai-Ling could continue living with her mother but Thuy had to live with her father? Should Mr. Pham have been required to attend an alcohol treatment program before Thuy lived with him? What about the questions that Judge Rivers asked Thuy? Do you think it was in her best interest to live with her father? Why or why not? If you were Judge Rivers, how would you have ruled in each case? Why? How would you feel if you were Ingrid? Should Judge Rivers have the power to require Mrs. Pham to deny her lesbian identity so she can see her own daughter? Do you think the judge abused his power?

No doubt you have strong feelings about both of these cases. It is important to realize that gay parents are often faced with child custody lawsuits based upon the nongay parent's homophobic fears, anger, and values. Equally important is the realization that a child's destiny depends on the personal biases and opinions of the judge in court that day. No one seemed to question Mr. Pham's drinking problem or his violent outbursts. No one asked whether or not Mrs. Pham was a loving, supportive mother. No one cared that Mr. Pham paid no child support and Thuy had lived in a one-room efficiency before they lived with Ingrid. Didn't the day-care teacher, the minister, and the court-appointed psychiatrist all say that Thuy was doing very well in school and was a delightful, well-adjusted child? Did anyone care that Mr. Pham had said during the divorce hearing that he had never even wanted children? Why didn't the judge ask Thuy any of those questions? Had Judge Rivers even heard her describe her father's violent outbursts and her fear when he was home? The only issue addressed by the court was whether or not Mrs. Pham, a lesbian, was a fit parent. Few parents flaunt their sexuality in front of their children. Why did Judge Rivers think that Mrs. Pham would inappropriately display her sexuality in front of Thuy but Mr. Pham would not?

HONESTY IS THE BEST POLICY

As difficult as it may be for a parent to tell his or her children about a gay life-style, the reactions of children to this often earth-shattering news is greatly varied. You may feel that your entire world has crumbled before your very eyes. The relationship you had with your gay parent and the type of parenting that existed previously has now been lost forever. Whether or not your new, more honest relationship is better or worse will depend on you.

If you take time to observe children of different ages coping with gay parents, it becomes obvious that when and if prejudices occur, society is usually the teacher. Otherwise, why should a six-year-old be able to deal with his parent's life-style with open arms and a twelve-year-old feel so threatened by it? The younger child reacts to the quality of parenting; if it is positive and supportive, parental acceptance is not a problem. Mark is a perfect example of proud acceptance.

Mark

Mark is six years old and lives with his dad, Joe, and his dad's friend, Stephen. He has been living with them since he was three. He sees a lot of his mom, and occasionally they all get together for pizza or to go to a football game. Mark remembers his dad talking to him over a year ago about different kinds of families. He didn't really care about knowing the names of all these families, but it seemed important to his dad at the time, so Mark tried very hard to listen. After all, if there is love and caring in a family, the name shouldn't matter. And there was no doubt in his mind that he had it all.

Mark's best friend, Timothy, had a family with one of those other names. He remembered his dad using Tim as an example, but he didn't remember the name. Mark really enjoyed being with Timothy, but he hated staying over at his house. His mom and dad yelled at each other all the time, and Timothy stayed in his room with the door closed to get away from all of the yelling.

In contrast, when Timothy came over to Mark's house or went with him to visit his mom, they had a wonderful time. Frequently, Joe and Stephen took the two of them on long bike rides, and often his mom drove them to the lake to feed the ducks and play. Mark wished that Timothy could come live with him and be his brother. He didn't mind being an only child, but he sure had more fun playing with Timothy.

Mark especially loved being with his family at school functions. When other children asked him why he had three parents, he simply said that he must be special— that all of them wanted to share him. It was no big deal to any of his classmates whether someone had one, two, three, or four parents.

The recent field day was the neatest event of the school year in Mark's opinion. Most parents that came just stood around talking. But his mom, dad, and Stephen all pitched in to help run things. He was so proud of them. However, he felt very sorry for Timothy; neither of his parents came, and he looked so sad and alone. Mark invited Timothy to picnic with his family, and Stephen held his hand and walked with him when Tim went up to receive his medal. It made Mark feel proud and secure to have parents who cared so much for his friend.

Which of these two families would you rather be a member of ? Notice that for Mark the words homosexual and heterosexual were not important enough even to remember. What was important to him were the feelings he had when he was with each type of family. Which child is more likely to grow up feeling like a worthwhile person? Which family would you want to live in? Why? When our society robs a child of this kind of acceptance, we certainly must question its intention. Who is the better teacher here, the child or society?

THE YOUNG AND THE RESTLESS

From a developmental standpoint, younger children have less trouble handling knowledge of a gay parent's life-style than do older children. They treat the details of their home lives matter-of-factly and without preconceived notions. Think back to how you would have described your family when you were four, six, eight, or ten. How did you feel about your family when you suddenly reached adolescence?

There is probably no time during which physical and emotional changes are as rapid or profound as they are during adolescence. Between the ages of twelve and twenty, you are trying to adjust to an entirely new body image and simultaneously developing new forms of relationships with other people. Early adolescence is the time in your life when conformity is most important, and the opinions of your peers take on greater importance than your parents' opinions. See what happens to J.D. and Tommy when their friends accuse their mother of being a lesbian.

J.D. and Tommy

The hustle and bustle of city life was finally too much for Sandi to handle. She wanted to raise her sons J.D. and Tommy, ages twelve and fourteen respectively, in an area where pollution and prejudice were minimal, the neighbors friendly, and the horses ran wild. The boys were excited about living on a ranch in Jackson Hole, Wyoming. For years Sandi had dreamed of buying, breaking, and selling horses the way her grandfather had described to her years ago. Both sons knew how to ride, and the idea thrilled all of them. But could they afford such a move at this time?

Being a single parent had never bothered Sandi, even though it was beginning to be difficult raising two teenage sons. The boys knew that they had an anonymous donor father but that she had wanted each of them very much. J.D. and Tommy admired their mother's numerous and diverse talents, as well as her determination to raise them in a world that gave her very little support. They knew from their earliest childhood memories that their mother was a lesbian, but they had never experienced any discrimination so it was no big deal. Little did they know what lay ahead of them in Wyoming.

As a computer technician and software developer, Sandi could pack up and move anywhere in the country and still retain her job. J.D. and Tommy had all the latest in computers and software, and their mother often tested new programs or games on them. Their computer skills far surpassed those of most adults, but J.D. and Tommy never made their friends feel inferior or stupid. Sandi had taught them well how to make and keep friends. As the current school year drew to a close, the three of them packed in anticipation of their move West.

The ranch they had purchased was fifteen miles outside of Jackson Hole and consisted of twenty-five acres. It was small in comparison to the ranches nearby, but it seemed huge to them. The house, barn, and corral were all in good shape, and someone even had a small garden plot established. J.D. had just turned thirteen, and by the time school started Tommy would be fifteen and could get a driver's permit.

It took the entire summer for them to settle in, find the grocery store and drugstore, and gradually meet their neighbors. Everyone seemed friendly and offered them lots of advice on how to get ready for the winter. It was hard to think that far in advance, but Sandi knew they were right as she looked out on the Teton Range every morning. J.D. and Tommy were thrilled to meet new friends. Tommy was beginning to be interested in dating girls, whereas J.D. was enthralled with the new computer game that his mother was designing.

Russell, who owned the largest ranch in the area and also broke horses, took Sandi under his wing and helped her purchase fifteen horses. J.D. and Tommy quickly began fighting over which horse belonged to each of them. At one point, Sandi found them wrestling in the barn.

Each morning the three of them had to get up at 5:30 to do the chores before school started. Sandi drove them to school and then returned home to work. It didn't take long, however, for Sandi to realize that she was going to need some help on the ranch. But whom could she trust, and did she want another man living on the ranch? Tommy was old enough now to feel like the man of the house. J.D. had a hard enough time taking orders from his older brother, so Sandi wasn't sure what she wanted to do.

The boys usually got a ride home with Reggie and Dallas. They would all retreat into the study where the computers were set up and spend an hour or so challenging each other on their problem-solving skills. One afternoon, Dallas took a picture off the bookcase and asked Tommy who was in the picture with his mother. Tommy thought quickly and said it was his Aunt Melanie. Then Reggie spotted another picture and asked who was in it. J.D. answered this time and said it was another aunt named Shirley. Suddenly Dallas was holding a book, and Tommy and J.D. froze. Dallas threw it to Reggie, who read the title out loud, *The Joy of Lesbian Sex*. Their "secret" had been discovered, and J.D. and Tommy didn't know what to expect.

All was quiet the next day at school, but J.D. and Tommy ate lunch alone in the cafeteria. It seemed as if everyone was talking *about* them, but no one wanted to talk *to* them. Fortunately, Tommy could now drive them to school and they didn't need to rely on Dallas and Reggie for a ride home. For three months their lives were miserable, but things started to improve around the holidays. That is, until Angel moved in with them.

Sandi had been interviewing people to help work the ranch, and she chose someone who could break horses gently, but quickly. Russell had given Angel a high recommendation, and that was good enough for Sandi. The boys were stunned when they arrived home from school and met Angel as she was moving into the small back bedroom. They knew better than to challenge their mother's decision.

J.D. and Tommy were grateful that they finally had some help with the horses in the mornings and at night. They watched in awe as Angel firmly but gently taught a horse to accept a bit, a bridle, a saddle, and eventually, a rider. The stories that Angel told at dinner were funny and captivating at the same time. They enjoyed being around Angel and saw a twinkle in their mother's eye that had been missing for a long time. Life was getting better on the open plains!

Over the weekend Sandi's car broke down. The boys didn't mind riding in Angel's pick-up truck, and she dropped them off on her way to the feed store. Three miles away from the school, Angel realized that the boys had left their lunches in the truck. She turned around and headed back to school. Classes had already started when she got there, so Angel dropped the lunches off in the office with the boys' names on them. The students just stared at her as she walked down the hall. Then Angel spotted Tommy at his locker and told him what she had done. As Angel disappeared around the corner, several of his friends asked who the guy was. Tommy just said, "One of my mom's friends." Throughout the day, the kids kept talking about whether Angel was a man or a woman. J.D. and Tommy never did eat the lunches.

It wasn't long after that day that the phone calls started in the middle of the night. Then the words "dyke" and "lesbian" appeared painted on the side of the barn. One morning they awoke to discover that the corral had been opened and all the horses were loose. What other punishments would they have to endure for being different?

How would you feel if you had an anonymous donor father? Why do you think Sandi chose to have two children rather than one? Did J.D. and Tommy seem well adjusted and normal? Why did Sandi think there would be less prejudice and pollution in Wyoming? If you were Tommy, would you have considered yourself the man of the house? If so, how would you have felt if Sandi had hired a male to break horses rather than a female?

It is hard for any child to move into a new home and develop new friendships. Would it have been fair for J.D. and Tommy to have asked their mother not to display embarrassing photographs and books in the house? How can Sandi acknowledge her lesbian identity with her sons at home and yet respect their privacy when having company? How should J.D. and Tommy deal with their mother's friend Angel? Should they tell their friends the truth, or is this a secret that should be kept?

The vast majority of research indicates that the adolescent years are the most traumatic for discovering a parent's gay identity. However, even when an adult discovers that a parent is gay, it can be a crisis. You may wonder whether the parent had known all along and just didn't tell you, or had just acknowledged it to himself or herself. A million questions bombard you, and the shock of the news precludes rational thinking. Let's walk these steps with Jacob and Marshall and see how they handled their parents' news.

Jacob

Jacob had been away at college for three years, but things had seemed normal enough when he came home on vacations. This summer, however, the atmosphere was one of silence, stress, and distance. His parents, Martha and Stanley, were rarely home at the same time, and when they were, the tension was almost unbearable. They didn't communicate much with each other, nor did they communicate much with him. Had he had done something to cause this? Was he in the way when he came home? He hated the silence most of all. He wished he could at least hear them argue; that way he would have some clue to what the problem was.

Jacob had been dating Barbara Jean for about four years, and they planned to get married when he finished college. He often talked with her about his concerns about his family. He still enjoyed being with each of them individually, but he was miserable when they were all together. Something was missing. It was as if pieces of the family unit had been lost or rearranged.

Then one weekend when his father was out of town, his mother told him she wanted to talk with him. When they sat down together, she seemed very nervous, which was completely out of character for her. Most people would have described Martha as a "pillar of strength." She was the heart and soul of the family and the person that everyone counted on. Jacob could feel a knot in the pit of his stomach. What was going on here, he thought.

Martha began by saying that what she was going to tell him would probably come as a total surprise and upset him. She assured Jacob that her only intent was to be honest with him. She said that the courage to have this conversation came from her love and respect for him as her son and now as a man. All she asked in return were his honest feelings. Martha also said that she had chosen to tell each of her children separately, so that their reactions would not be influenced by each other. At this point Jacob was convinced that his mother was going to tell him she had some terminal disease. Instead, she simply said, "Jacob, I am a lesbian."

Shock hardly describes his reaction. Not **my** mom, he thought. For a moment, he wished she *had* said she had an incurable disease; he could understand that more easily. Jacob's head was spinning as his mother continued talking.

Martha explained that she had been struggling with her feelings since she was a teenager and had finally reached the point of acknowledging her lesbian identity. She had told Stanley in May, and he was obviously having great difficulty accepting it. Jacob asked if they would be separating and divorcing. She nodded yes, and the tears welled up in her eyes. Stanley had told her to pack her bags and get out by July 1st.

As they stood up, Martha hugged him tightly and said, "I love you very much, and you will always be an integral part of my life, no matter where I am." They agreed to talk again later in the week when Jacob had had a chance to sort out his feelings.

Jacob left the house and drove to the beach. He needed time to be alone and think. Would he have to tell his friends? If so, how would he tell them? How would his brother and sister react? At this moment, he felt a sense of anger that his family of twenty-one years would be broken up. But at the same time, he felt sorry for his mother; she seemed so alone as she faced him with the news. He felt uncomfortable and incapable of accepting his own mother as a lesbian.

In a strange way, Jacob also felt enormous respect for this wonderful woman who had given him so much of herself. How could she love him so much and yet risk losing him? Was she any different today than she was yesterday when she was not a lesbian in his eyes?

Jacob thought of the discussions he and Barbara Jean were having about children. Could he, as a parent, ever demonstrate such courage and love for his children in an effort to be truthful about something? He could hardly imagine such deep devotion. Crazy thoughts and feelings were running rampant through his mind when he realized the depth of caring his mother had just modeled. He looked up at the stars and whispered, "Thank you, Mom, I love you too."

Marshall

All his life Marshall had wanted to be a professional musician like his father, Ian. Few people could play the keyboard as well as his father. Ian had perfect pitch and played everything by ear. If someone hummed a few bars of a tune, he could play the full accompaniment. Marshall loved to hang out at the clubs with his father and the boys in the band. Unfortunately, his classmates thought his dad was "one of the boys." At first, he didn't know what they meant by that. But before long he couldn't stop some of his classmates from shouting "fag" or "fairy" without a fight. Marshall's mother was worried about his getting hurt, but no one was going to call his father gay and get away with it.

Marshall persuaded his parents to buy him a guitar for Christmas when he was fourteen. He spent every free minute practicing. He imitated what he heard on the radio or stereo. Joker Joe, the lead guitarist in his father's band, taught him how to bar chords and play rhythm guitar. Ian treasured the time he spent with his son, but he knew he needed to encourage Marshall to attend a college with an excellent music program. Ian considered his son extremely talented in music.

Unlike his two brothers, Marshall preferred music to sports. He had a slight build and wore his hair long. Even his brothers called him a fag, but only in jest. Marshall tried not to let it bother him, but it did. The worst part, though, was persuading girls to date him. Marshall felt very comfortable with his sexual identity and considered his long hair simply a statement of his individuality, not his sexual orientation. Didn't his father have short hair and they still called him a fag?

The years flew by as Marshall pursued a music major at the University of Illinois. His graduation recital was a center-stage performance at the Krannert Center. He still remembered how he had felt as a freshman when he entered this magnificent performing center. His family, especially his father, were in the audience when he played that afternoon.

His music degree and the education he had received traveling with his father's band enabled Marshall to decide how he wanted to use his musical ability. He wanted to be in the Hollywood entertainment industry, and he hoped to audition for several of the bands that provided music for television talk shows. After months of auditions, Marshall was offered a temporary position with the band on a network television show and would be leaving home at the end of the week. His family were bursting with pride, and his father asked him to play with his own band the Saturday before he was to leave. Marshall was both humbled and honored by this request. Even his brothers Nathan and Edward began to brag about their "baby" brother.

On Saturday the band played before a full house that brought them back for two encores. There was a lot of back-slapping and high fives, and the mood was jovial. Marshall's friends started making jokes about the kind of people in Hollywood and told him he had to be careful. He was sick of hearing comments about getting AIDS, but he smiled and passed off the remarks.

Marshall packed up his instruments and sat down alone with his father for the first time in years. They spoke about the good old days and the adventure he was about to embark upon. Suddenly, Ian grew very quiet. After a moment's hesitation, he said, "Son, you know all these years your friends have called me gay? Well, I have been gay all my life. Your mother knew but made me promise not to tell. Now that you're a man, I thought you should know."

Marshall sprang out of his chair, knocking it over. "You're what?" he shouted. "You son of a bitch! All those years I defended you. I had the crap kicked out of me more times than I can count. You lied to me, and I bet you lied to my mother so no one would ever really know you were a fag. I don't ever want to see you again." With

that tirade, Marshall shoved Ian off his chair and ran out
of the club with tears streaming down his face.

Whose reaction can you identify with more, Jacob's or
Marshall's? Each was an adult when he discovered that a
parent was gay. Do you think they were equally surprised, or do you think Marshall might have questioned
his father's sexual identity for a long time and simply
denied it? Was Marshall's reaction justified by the years
he had defended his father? Why did Jacob's father tell
Martha to pack her bags and get out, but Marshall's
mother continued living with Ian? If you were married
and had children and your spouse said that he or she was
gay, how would you react? In time, do you think Marshall
will see his father again, or has this news ended their
relationship forever? Would you terminate your relationship with a gay parent forever? Why or why not?

IS IT WORTH THE RISK TO TELL?

Parents never can know what your reaction to their gay or
lesbian identity will be. Some children respond with open
arms, with understanding and gratitude for their parents'
honesty. Parents often feel relieved when their children
know who they really are. But many children are overwhelmed and burdened with the news of a parent's gay
identity. These children may feel resentment, anger, and
even hatred for the parent. How would you react to news
of your parent's gay or lesbian identity?

Unlike telling a friend that your parents are divorced or
that one of them has died, you will probably get very little
support if you tell a friend that a parent is gay. You may
need to find a support group for yourself so you can air

your feelings. Therapy has helped many children deal with the problems associated with having a gay parent.

As we move to the next chapter, there are two questions that you need to answer. Was it worth the risk for your gay parent to be honest with you? Do you still love him or her as much as he or she loves you?

CHAPTER ◇ 5

Living in a
"Catch-22"

A "Catch-22" situation might be described as one in which there is no obvious solution, no real winner. When lives are interwoven and one small part begins to move, the result is a domino effect. The entire family structure begins to change shape. The fact that the change may be made for good reasons does little to lessen the discomfort of the people involved. When any one family member feels that the reasons for change are not valid, there is tremendous resistance and negative reaction to that change. Who suffers in a family varies from case to case. Let's begin by observing a situation in which the child is in a Catch-22.

Nancy

As far as Nancy knew, she was the product of a middle-class, Caucasian, heterosexual family. She was aware that some children were raised in homosexual families because that had been a topic of discussion in health class during her junior year. However, she never associated any of what was described with either of her parents. She had noticed that her dad didn't seem like the energetic, jovial person he used to be, but she attributed that to the pressure she knew he was under at work.

The summer between her junior and senior years, her father, Forrest, moved out. She remembers it vividly. The day before he left, he had called from work to ask Nancy if he could talk to her privately when he came home. She wondered what he had to tell her. Had he gotten a promotion? Was he going to change jobs? Was he sick? She hoped and prayed that nothing was wrong.

During the afternoon, while Nancy was in the garage doing laundry, she heard someone come in the front door. Much to her surprise, her mother appeared and asked if they could talk. Nancy knew immediately that something was seriously wrong. What was happening to this family? Why weren't they all talking together?

Nancy and her mother sat down at the kitchen table. It was obvious that her mother was extremely angry and upset. With no preparation, she blurted out, "Your father is gay, and he is leaving us tomorrow." Nancy was stunned. She didn't know whether to try to deal with her mother's anger and emotionality or with the news about her father. Could her mother be telling the truth? Was her father going to tell her that he was gay, or just that he was leaving?

Nancy's mother went on and on about what a pervert her father was and how sinful his choice of a life-style was. Nancy didn't know whether to agree with her mother so as to console her or not. She didn't want to judge her father until they had talked. She could hardly imagine facing him now. Nancy wasn't sure at this point what her mother's intentions were. Was she simply trying to inform

Nancy that her father was gay, or was she trying to turn her against her father? Nancy was relieved when her mother left the house, saying that she wanted to talk with her friend Marilyn. Nancy needed time alone to process the news and think about her own feelings.

In what seemed like a few minutes, her father came home. Strangely, he seemed more relaxed and less anxious than her mother. How could that be? Did he not realize the impact of his disclosure, or was he relieved to acknowledge it?

They too sat down in the kitchen, and Forrest held both her hands in his. Taking a deep breath, he calmly revealed his gay identity to Nancy. Forrest told her that he was honored to be her father and that he loved her more than anything. His voice cracked and his eyes filled with tears, but he never lost control. His greatest concern was the hurt this revelation would bring to her. The pain in his eyes and his body language convinced her of his sincerity. Forrest told her he would be moving into an apartment the next day and wanted to hear from her when she was ready.

In the following weeks, Nancy paid a high price for visiting her father. She worried about his living alone and being lonely, but she also needed for him to answer a hundred questions. After each visit, she had to withstand her mother's wrath. Nancy was in a no-win situation. She disagreed with her mother's reaction and began to withdraw as her mother vented her anger with hurtful accusations. She loved both of her parents very much and did not want to have to choose sides.

How would you react as the middle person in this situation? Could you stand your ground with your mother and still remain respectful? Why is Nancy supportive of her father's move? Is this a situation that could drive you to leave home? How can Nancy maintain her own integrity and a relationship with each parent without losing the other parent? Can you see why we say Nancy is in a Catch-22?

"TO GRANDMOTHER'S HOUSE WE GO"...

Given the wrong circumstances, the ho-ho-ho of the Christmas season can become the horror of the holidays. Traditionally, the holidays bring out emotions and feelings that are strangely tucked away the rest of the year. Statistically, more suicides occur during the holidays than at any other time. It is not surprising, then, that these times of special family gatherings put tremendous pressure on the person who no longer "fits" into the family unit. This trap affords us a look at another Catch-22 example.

Holidays routinely force people to make decisions— decisions about gifts, schedules, and people. What can I give this person that will be special? When will I see the people from out of town? If my schedule is a problem, how do I choose whom to see without hurting anyone's feelings? How can a person be expected to relax and enjoy the holidays facing such dilemmas? The agony of the holidays is obvious as we spend time with Marcia.

Marcia

The Christmas holidays were the highlight of Marcia's year. Decorating the tree, putting up lights in the yard, and baking cookies were traditions that she looked forward to all year. Her entire family was really into the meaning of this season. Even David, her older brother, and Susan, the eldest, were delighted to spend the evenings before Christmas stringing popcorn and cranberries for the tree while listening to Christmas carols. There was a feeling of contentment, joy, and togetherness within the house.

The Christmas season was always peaceful and loving until Marcia's parents divorced. The split was more congenial than she would have expected, and for months that made life easier. David and Susan now had their own families and lived in Colorado. Mom and Dad had explained to her that she was in no way responsible for their split. They simply were no longer compatible as husband and wife.

Marcia missed seeing both of her parents every day, but she was relieved to see each of them interacting happily with other people. Her mother's eyes had a new twinkle, especially when she and her friend Ioko were together. In many ways, her mother seemed more self-confident, and Ioko brought out some of her mother's best qualities. With the gentle prodding of Ioko, her mother attended the local community college and took a computer class. An accomplished pianist, Ioko gave her mother piano lessons in exchange for using her washer and dryer twice a week. Marcia enjoyed seeing the barter system that these two women had worked out. If only her father would find someone to bring joy into his life again.

As the Christmas season approached, it became obvious to Marcia that her parents had no intention of getting together for a family dinner. This forced her to face a very painful decision: Whom would she spend Christmas with? Did the holiday mean more to one parent than the other? Why couldn't they all be together for this one day? Couldn't they see the pain and anguish they were causing her? Why did this have to happen to her now when David and Susan weren't around? Marcia resented both of her parents for putting her in this position and robbing her of the joy of Christmas. She wondered if she would always associate Christmas with unhappiness and her parents' divorce.

In the midst of the turmoil, Marcia suddenly realized that there was only one person in the world she could spend Christmas with and have it feel like it used to: her grandmother. In that way she wouldn't have to make the choice; her parents would. Whether or not they wanted to share Christmas with her and her grandmother was their decision. To make it even better, she knew her grandmother would love the idea. Marcia could hardly wait to call her.

The excitement in her grandmother's voice assured Marcia that she had made the right decision. She explained her predicament and waited to hear agreement from the other end of the line. To her amazement, her grandmother responded, "Marcia, you know you will always be welcome in my home. However, your mother the lesbian is not. I will not be disgraced by her presence." Marcia was astounded by her grandmother's words. What did she mean, her "lesbian mother"? No such thing existed in her family. Her mom was a happy, outgoing, well-adjusted woman. Was Grandmother getting senile?

Her grandmother went on that the gossip was all over town about the lesbian relationship between Marcia's mother and Ioko. She ranted and raved about how the family name had been ruined, how selfish Marcia's mother was, and how disappointing it was to have such a daughter. She even went so far as to suggest that Marcia consider living with her, or perhaps with her father.

How could anyone think about Christmas? As people focused on a special birth, Marcia could think of nothing but death. Suicide had to be easier than the choices she now faced in life. Was her mother's lesbianism the reason David and Susan moved to another state, or was that coincidental?

Do you think Marcia ever saw another Christmas? Should Marcia ask her father if he had heard the rumor about her mother and Ioko? How should Marcia approach her mother about the accusation? If her mother is a lesbian, how will that change Marcia's Christmas plans? Is there any way for Marcia's mother to convince her own mother that she is not a lesbian? If you were Marcia's mother, how would you feel if your own mother deserted you? How would you ask a parent if he or she was gay?

We have seen a season of laughter and joy turn into one of anguish and hopelessness. Should an alternate life-style have such dread consequences? Isn't that a high price to pay for loving and caring for someone of the same gender? If you were Marcia's best friend and she confided in you that her mother was lesbian, how would you persuade her not to commit suicide?

Bryan and Anthony

Bryan and Anthony were eleven-year-old identical twins. No one could tell them apart if they were dressed the same. They enjoyed switching classes at school and playing pranks on the school secretary. When their parents were married, their mother had always dressed them alike. It robbed them of their individuality, but their mother thought they looked cute. After the divorce, however, their father Derrick said that all of them needed a "new look," and each of them chose his own clothes from that day on. Maybe living with their father would be "in the boys' best interest," as the judge had said.

As a chemical engineer, Derrick worked on numerous environmental projects. Bryan hoped to follow in his father's footsteps, while Anthony wanted to become a nurse-midwife. He loved children and wanted to bring babies into the world, but he didn't enjoy studying enough to spend seven long years in medical school. Derrick told each of them to "follow his heart, work very hard, and treat all people with love and respect." Bryan and Anthony always made faces when their father recited this line, but they knew he tried to live by this golden rule.

Only one thing really bothered them about living with their father. Before the divorce, when their parents had company for dinner, Bryan and Anthony were allowed to sit with the company. They had good table manners and knew never to interrupt the dinner conversation. Now that they were living with their father, they had to eat in their bedroom or the kitchen when Derrick had company for dinner. Was their father embarassed by them? Didn't any of his new friends have children? What were Derrick and his friends talking about that was inappropriate for them to hear? Didn't he trust them to meet his friends?

While Bryan and Anthony were questioning their father's behavior, Derrick was also questioning it. The divorce was on the grounds of habitual drunkeness; his ex-wife was an alcoholic. But Derrick had been wondering about his own sexual orientation since he was ten. He had been seeing a therapist for years, and they agreed that he was bisexual. Derrick was faithful to his wife during the marriage, but he never felt that she met all his physical and emotional needs. Which meant that he was now dating a man named Aaron. Even though his sons were only eleven, they were beginning to discover that they had sexual feelings, and Derrick was concerned about exhibiting any sexual behavior in front of them. It was extremely important to Derrick that Bryan and Anthony never feel uncomfortable with his gay or bisexual friends.

Can you see the Catch-22 that Bryan and Anthony are in? They feel that their father is embarassed by them, and their father doesn't want his behavior to embarass his sons. How can the three of them overcome this communication problem? Are the boys old enough to be told about Derrick's life-style? Should Derrick ask his friends to refrain from any behavior that might be misinterpreted as sexual by his sons?

It's important to realize that when men get together for dinner, no one openly displays sexuality. Adults, both gay and nongay, know when sexual behavior is appropriate and when it is not. Bryan and Anthony will be robbed of an important part of their development if they are barred from interacting with gay or bisexual men. It is through this interaction that they will learn to accept people for who they are, not who attracts them sexually.

JEOPARDY

What do you think of when you hear the word intimacy? Unconditional love? Security? Sex? Happiness? For many people, those words describe their feelings for and relationship with their partner. For others, however, intimacy is synonymous with being slapped, punched, bitten, stabbed, burned, or shot. If you ask any police officer what type of call is the most dangerous to respond to, without hesitating the officer would reply domestic violence. We live in a society that condones aggressive-

ness, especially in males, and encourages us to be aggressive to "get ahead."

Our laws protect us from assault by strangers, but loved
ones are allowed to be violent when they are angry.
Violence may be seen as a continuum, with "normal"
abuse (such as spanking a child) at one end and violence
(such as hitting and stabbing) at the other. Think back to
your own childhood. Who was the disciplinarian when
you did something wrong? How were you disciplined?
Were you sent to your room? Did you have privileges
taken away, such as the television, computer, telephone,
or going out with your friends? Were you spanked reason-
ably for the offense, or did you perceive the punishment
as a form of physical abuse or violence? How were your
closest friends punished by their parents? Did you think
you were fairly disciplined in comparison?

It was not easy for your parents to decide what type of
punishment would deter you from misbehaving. But what
happens when you see one of your parents being physically
abused by the other? Keith and Dee Dee find themselves
in that dilemma and face a Catch-22 that they don't know
how to handle. What would you do in their shoes?

Keith and Dee Dee

After living alone with their father in Wisconsin for more
than four years, Keith and Dee Dee were thrilled when
their father was transferred to Seaside, Oregon. At age
twelve, Keith enjoyed fishing, hiking, and surfing with his
father while nine-year-old Dee Dee stayed with their
neighbor, Betty. Jason was proud of Keith's love of the
outdoors and tried to spend as much time as possible with
his son. Their mother's death had been harder on Keith
than on Dee Dee, but both children seemed to be adjust-

ing well, and they loved the Oregon coast as much as he did.

Jason had always wanted children and knew he would be a great parent, but he could never shake his attraction to men. He had met Pablo in a surfing contest over a year earlier and had been dating him ever since. Jason talked freely about his adventures with Pablo, and the children soon begged to be included on the weekends. Gradually, Pablo became part of the family and had dinner with them one or two nights during the week. Dee Dee was spellbound by Pablo's stories about the war in the Persian Gulf, and she enjoyed his bedtime stories. Keith, however, missed the quiet time he had spent alone with his father. It seemed as if Pablo was always with them, and Keith was both jealous and hurt that his father included Pablo on their outings.

After Jason and Pablo had been dating for more than two years, they began talking about living together. Their main concern was the children. How would Keith and Dee Dee react? Jason had one other concern that he never shared with Pablo: Pablo's explosive and often violent temper. If a driver cut him off passing or changing lanes, Pablo swore vehemently and pounded on the steering wheel. When the two of them had a disagreement, Pablo would put his face two inches from Jason's and yell at Jason to hit him. Sometimes it escalated to a shoving match, but Jason usually just walked away until Pablo calmed down. How would they handle their disagreements in front of the children? Jason was not sure he wanted to live with Pablo, but he knew he loved him very much.

The transfer to Oregon had given Jason a lot more responsibility in his company, but he loved working with people and his coworkers respected him. One evening he arrived home a little later than usual and found Pablo already there with the children. Jason was stunned to learn that the lease on Pablo's apartment had not been renewed and he had ten days to find a new place to live. Dee Dee begged Jason to let Pablo move into the spare bedroom, and even Keith supported the request. With his head spinning and his doubts increasing, Jason heard himself say that Pablo was welcome to move in on the weekend. Later that might, Jason prayed that it was the right decision. Only time would tell.

During the first months, everyone was adjusting to having another person in the house. The conflicts were minor and normal: Who takes out the trash, does the laundry, cooks dinner? Keith seemed less threatened by Pablo's presence and actually enjoyed having another man around when his father was busy. Jason began traveling on his job and spent one night a month away from home. It was on one such occasion that Pablo's temper exploded.

Keith had two of his friends over after school, and they went into the gameroom to play. One of the boys picked up Pablo's baseball trophy from the mantel and accidentally dropped it. It shattered, and the boys quickly left. As Keith began explaining what had happened, Pablo went into a rage and started beating him. By the time he regained his composure, Keith had two black eyes, a bloody nose, and multiple bruises. Keith ran to his bedroom and locked the door. The next morning, Pablo came to his room and apologized. He promised never to hit Keith again and said he didn't know what had come over him. Keith stayed home from school and wondered what he could tell his father. Should he tell the truth or say he had gotten in a fight at school? Would his father also be mad at him for breaking Pablo's trophy, or would he understand? Keith decided that lying would save everyone more pain; especially himself.

Jason returned tired but pleased with his business meetings. He had procured several contracts for his company and hoped the commission would allow all of them to take a much-needed vacation. When he saw Keith he was shocked. "What happened to you?" he asked. Keith mumbled something about a fight at school and promised it would never happen again. Jason sat down on his son's bed and told him that fighting never settled anything and that words and education were much more powerful weapons. He hugged Keith closely and said, "I love you, son." Jason left the room, but he had a nagging feeling in the pit of his stomach.

Not long afterward, Pablo and Jason got into a fight after attending a concert. Pablo had been given a speeding ticket on the way home, and he blamed the speedometer in Jason's car. They were shouting at each other as they walked into the house, and the children woke up to see Pablo pushing and slapping their father around. Jason put his hands up to protect himself, and Pablo decked him. Dee Dee began crying hysterically, and Jason quickly picked her up and said they were just playing. "Men play differently than children," he said. Keith just glared from the staircase and prayed that his father would be okay.

The violent outbursts became more frequent, but they were always directed at Jason, never the children. They fought over the car, money, their friends, and sometimes the children. Pablo was bigger and stronger than Jason, but it was Jason's house. Keith wondered why his father didn't fight back, call the police, or throw Pablo out. What would you have done if you were Jason?

*   *   *

There are several Catch-22s in this situation. First, Keith and Dee Dee want their father to be happy, but at the same time they want Pablo to stop hitting him. Second, Keith and Dee Dee were the ones who invited Pablo to live with them. Should they also be responsible for telling Pablo to move out? Third, all of them enjoy being with Pablo when his temper is under control. Should they suggest therapy and ask Pablo to change? How would you feel if you were Pablo? How would you feel if you were Keith and Dee Dee?

No family is immune from violence and abuse. Healthy, functional families, however, know how to channel their anger. They use conflict as a tool for change and growth. How does your family handle conflict? As we look inside another family, you will see that violence and abuse often take on a different, more subtle appearance. Let's meet Reggie.

Reggie

Reggie had been sexually abused by his father for years. No one knew exactly how long the abuse had gone on because whenever his mother, Kelly, asked Reggie about the "games" his father played with him, Reggie became silent and withdrawn. His grandparents arrived unexpectedly one day, and the next thing he knew, Reggie was celebrating his seventh birthday in Cologne, Germany. His mother filed for divorce, and the German courts said that his father could not see him. For the first time in his life, Reggie was safe.

Everything about Germany fascinated him. He knew from school that "the wall" had fallen and East and West Germany were struggling to become unified. Reggie wanted to see all the places that he had studied about last year. They were in Berlin when his mother met Gaby. Unlike many of his mother's other friends, Reggie liked Gaby immediately. She was tall and athletic, and her curiosity about America caused hours of questions and laughter. In exchange, Gaby became their guide and interpreter. Reggie worked very hard learning German and could communicate easily in less than a year. His grammar was far from perfect, but everyone could understand him.

After two and a half years in Germany, the divorce was final and his mother was granted sole custody. Just as Reggie's life seemed so calm and serene, his mother said that they would be flying back to the United States at the end of the week. How could they just walk away from Gaby? He loved her like a second mother and wanted her to join them. Why did they have to leave now?

Unbeknownst to Reggie, his grandparents had given their daughter an ultimatum: Either end her lesbian relationship with Gaby or they would petition the German courts for custody of Reggie. Kelly and Gaby had spent many hours discussing what was in Reggie's best interest, and they decided that living in the United States would allow him to have greater contact with his extended family. So Kelly and Reggie flew to Washington, D.C. to start their life over again. Gaby promised to write and said she would try to join them. Reggie never saw her again, and his heart was broken.

Washington was a fascinating place for a ten-year-old, but his mother wasn't around very much. Kelly became heavily involved in politics and became a gay rights activist. Reggie wasn't sure what it meant to have a lesbian mother, but at least he met lots of other children whose parents were gay. The year passed slowly, as he received only one letter from Gaby and two postcards from his grandparents. Everyone had been so friendly in Germany. Why had these people turned their backs on him?

His mother began taking him to meetings with other lesbians. He was placed in their care while she met with politicians behind closed doors. It was during these times that Reggie became the victim of extreme verbal abuse from some of these women. Though others were kind to him, these hostile women scared and confused him by their anger. He had just turned eleven. How could he be a threat to them, and did they really want to harm him because he was a male?

How would you feel if you were Reggie? Would you have asked your mother why you had to leave Germany? Do you think Reggie's grandparents treated him fairly? If you were Kelly's parents and found out that your daughter was in a loving lesbian relationship, would you have threatened to take Reggie away from her? Why or why not?

Have you figured out the Catch-22 that Reggie is in? His mother is very happy as a gay activist, and she trusted some of her closest friends to take care of Reggie. How would she feel if she knew that her friends were verbally abusing Reggie? If you were Reggie, would you tell your mother about the abuse or handle it by yourself?

Children are often trapped in a Catch-22 and don't know how to get out of it. Sometimes they are trying to protect a parent from getting hurt and other times they are trying to protect themselves. Take a few minutes and think about your parent's partner. Has he or she ever been abusive toward you or your parent? If so, how did you handle it? Did you remain silent and suffer the abuse because you loved your parent, or did you go to your parent and ask for help? If you suffered in silence, is it also possible that your parent has suffered in silence for you? Maybe you are both caught in a Catch-22!

POMP AND CIRCUMSTANCE

The emotions involved in any graduation experience are numerous. The contrast of feelings is probably never more prevalent. First, there is joy over the accomplishment of finishing. Second, there is sadness about leaving close and dear friends. Third, it marks a beginning as well as an end. Last, but not least, it is a time of celebration and also one of serious contemplation. It causes you to look back with pride and often to look ahead with some degree of fear and anxiety. Certainly, any combination of these emotions is difficult to handle. Any one of them is a Catch-22 situation. Just imagine compounding the problem in the following circumstances.

Jeffrey's Dilemma

Jeffrey had given college his best and gotten the best from it in return. He attributed part of that success to the confidence he had felt when he arrived on campus. He had graduated from high school ranked second in his class of 450 students. He had been active in a wide range of activities and felt respected and supported by his classmates and teachers.

Jeff lived with his father, Drew, and Drew's partner, Chris. They had lived together for about eight years. Jeff fondly remembered his high school graduation. Everyone was there: his mom, his grandmother, his older brother and sister, and of course his dad and Chris.

Actually, Jeffrey saw more of his brother and sister than of his mom. She was a sales representative for a pharmaceutical company and traveled extensively. Their time together was rare, brief, and very distant. However, she did volunteer to pay half of his college tuition, and that meant a lot to Jeff.

A couple of weeks before his tuition was due, Jeff's father lost his job at the navy yard. Rather than give the employees any severance pay, the government offered vocational training for new jobs. This meant that Drew had no income, and it would take six months to two years of training before he could qualify to find a new, non-governmental position. How would this affect Jeffrey's college education? Jeff had worked and saved some money, but not enough to make up the difference. The only sure thing he had now was his mother's half of the tuition and a work/study guarantee at college that assured him of only $350 per semester. Without a job, Drew couldn't borrow for Jeffrey's tuition. Meanwhile, Jeff was asking himself if it was fair to put his father in this position. Should he offer to work for a year and save money for his own education? Would it be easier on his father if he just enlisted in the Marines and skipped college altogether?

The week after his father learned of his termination, Drew, Chris, and Jeff were sitting at the table having dinner. When they had finished, Chris folded his napkin, pushed his chair back, and said to Jeff, "I want to ask a favor of you and your father. I have never had the wonderful experience of having a son of my own. However, I have been blessed with the opportunity to share you with your dad. I would consider it an honor to be permitted to pay half of your freshman year tuition." Jeff was stunned. He glanced at his father and saw tears well up in his eyes. Drew spoke first, asking if he and Jeff could have time to talk about it. They thanked Chris for his generous offer, and they all agreed to talk later in the week. As Chris stood up to clear his dishes, Jeff gave him a hug, and said "I love you."

Drew and Jeff did in fact accept Chris's offer. Jeffrey's freshman year was filled with success in every way. How could he ever thank Chris? Not only did he help secure his education financially, but his support, along with that of his dad, grandmother, brother, and sister, meant more than he could ever put a price tag on. Chris was a very important part of Jeffrey's family.

Drew and Chris attended every college activity they could free themselves for: soccer and football games, father/son trips, parent weekend, fraternity projects. Jeff loved having them there to meet his friends and share such special occasions. His friends accepted both men, and looked forward to their visits. Drew visited his son alone at least once a semester, but so did Chris. Those individual visits allowed growth in a very personal and special way for each of them.

Much like high school, the four years of college flew by. Before he knew it, graduation was a reality. But now the situation was different. He had access to only four tickets for his immediate family, but he needed five. Jeff asked all of his friends if anyone had an extra ticket. No one had enough for his or her own family, least of all an extra one.

Finally, Jeff found an extra ticket, but his relief was short-lived: what about his mother? He knew she loved him, but where did she fit in? Whom could he eliminate if he had to add her to his list? Soon it was obvious that it was a choice between Chris and his mom. Did he decide based upon feelings or obligation? He had shared so much more of his life with Chris, but she **was** his mother. Furthermore, she had no idea that Chris had paid the other half of his freshman year tuition.

Is this a Catch-22 or not? Would you eliminate your mother or tell her that Chris helped make possible the beginning of your college education? Would you give the ticket to your mom and hope Chris would understand? If Jeffrey's mother had not paid for half of his college education, would he even be in this situation? How would you feel if you were left out of Jeff's graduation after coparenting him through the years? Five tickets—six people—how would you handle it?

THE PLAGUE OF THE 1990s

Throughout history, humankind has been plagued by dread diseases that have aroused irrational fears and prejudices. Victims of these diseases could expect to be abandoned by some family members and friends, poorly treated by members of the medical community, and ostracized by society in general. Religious zealots often attributed these epidemics to God's wrath and just punishment for immorality and sin. These accusations were often accepted as truth because we lacked any scientific knowledge of the cause and nature of infectious diseases.

As early as 4000 B.C. in Egypt, leprosy evoked the same response, as did Antonine plague (measles) in classical Rome; syphilis and bubonic plague in medieval Europe; cholera, yellow fever, smallpox, and tuberculosis in eighteenth- and nineteenth-century Europe and North America; and influenza, polio, and Legionnaire's disease in twentieth-century America. How were these diseases dealt with? At first, people denied the reality of the disease. When people started dying in large numbers, a scapegoat had to be found so the blame could be placed somewhere. Victims sought relief from the medical community, which often included herbs or drugs that had not been tested or proven effective. When that failed to curb the number of deaths, carriers were isolated until society understood the mechanisms of the disease more clearly. Meanwhile, people were still dying.

What have we learned about dealing with epidemics over the past 6,000 years? As we look at the reactions of many Americans to AIDS, not very much. Former Surgeon General C. Everett Koop said, "AIDS has brought fear to the hearts of most Americans—fear of disease and fear of the unknown . . . Fear can be useful when it helps people avoid behavior that puts them at risk . . . unreasonable fear can be as crippling as the disease itself." What thoughts run through your head when you hear the word AIDS?

The plague of the 1990s is AIDS. You may be dealing with a parent who is asymptomatic and HIV-positive or who has full-blown AIDS. What does it mean if someone is asymptomatic but positive for the virus? It means that the person is currently healthy, but that his or her body has produced antibodies against the HIV (human immunodeficiency virus) infection. With our current knowledge, people with full-blown AIDS will, in time, die of some type of infection or cancer. According to researchers, a vaccine against the AIDS virus is still a long way off. They do predict, however, that in the not too distant future each of us will know someone who is HIV-positive. It's your turn to meet some people who are dealing with the ramifications of this plague in the '90s.

Mary Ann

"I am thirteen years old now. Whe I was three, my mom had another child, but Paul was born with severe birth defects and died before he could ever leave the hospital. Eighteen months after Paul died, Mom was pregnant again. We were all excited and started choosing names. Unfortunately, this time she had a miscarriage. They never tried to have another child, and I understand. It took all of us a long time to recover from those two tragedies.

"My parents have been divorced for over five years, and I live with my father. The relationship between my parents is pretty good, but we frequently fight when we all get together, so we don't do it very often.

"My parents met in junior high school and went steady all during high school and college. Dad eventually went on to become an orthopedic surgeon. Mom was the artistic one in the family and attended a fashion design school. The early years of their marriage were difficult, but everyone thought they were happy. No one questioned the sacrifices that Mom made in her career to put Dad through medical school. In our religion, wives are supposed to support their husbands and take care of the children. For a while, Mom was content with this arrangement, but as she met more people in the fashion design industry, she longed for more freedom.

"Living with two career-oriented parents was very difficult. As they began drifting apart, I spent more time with my paternal grandparents. On a return trip from New York, my mother burst into the house out of breath with packages in her arms from Paris and Rome. 'Guess what?' she said. 'I have been promoted to fashion design editor and I start in two weeks.' Neither of us knew what to say when she proposed that we move to New York. My father had just joined a prestigious medical practice in the Salt Lake City area, and he had no intention of leaving at this point in his career. Unbeknownst to us, Mom had already rented an apartment and was leaving for New York whether or not we joined her. So when they separated, there wasn't much discussion about with whom I would live.

"Trying to adjust to the hours of a renowned surgeon was very difficult for me. My father missed more recitals, plays, and PTA meetings than most single parents. But he also helped me with my homework, brushed my hair every night (that is, when he was home), and cooked wonderful meals. I enjoyed all of his friends, especially Dr. McIntyre and Dr. Hoffman. On weekends Dr. McIntyre (Lee) would pack a picnic basket and take me for a ride on his motorcycle around the lake while Dad worked. It was almost like having two fathers, but he had his own apartment about three miles from our house. Dr. Hoffman (Melanie) was beyond description: gullible, an awful cook, and very sensitive. Melanie was the perfect pediatric oncologist, as she related to children so well. In many ways, she became my surrogate mother. Overall, the four of us became one big, happy family.

"A month before my tenth birthday, my father said he needed to attend a conference and would be gone for a week. It was business as usual, and Melanie stayed with me. I was looking forward to my motorcycle ride with Lee, but he went with my father to the conference. They routinely went to conferences together, so I wasn't worried. I never expected the news I received when they returned.

"As my father sat down in his lounge chair, I noticed how frail and tired he looked. He asked me to sit in his chair with him so we could have a serious discussion. Lee and Melanie were with us when he told me that he had found out nine months earlier that he was HIV-positive. He and Lee had gone to the mountains for one last camping trip, and my father had figured out what to get me for my birthday.

"Nothing could have prepared me for my present. My father had bought me a one-way airplane ticket to New York so I could live with my mother! I began to scream and shake, and my father held me close. In a soothing voice, he told me that he was going to die and that he didn't want me to see him waste away. The four of us just held hands and cried uncontrollably for hours."

Although MaryAnn was only ten years old, she knew she wanted to live with her father until the moment he died. She didn't care how he looked before he died, as she loved him wholeheartedly. But at the same time, she didn't want her father to worry about her when he was dying. MaryAnn wanted to fulfill her dying father's wishes, but she didn't want him to be alone. Can you see the Catch-22 predicament that she was in?

What would you have done if you were MaryAnn? Why? Would MaryAnn fit into her mother's life-style easily? What changes would her mother have to make? Where would MaryAnn live if her mother didn't want her? How would Melanie and Lee feel if MaryAnn went to New York? Could they gain custody of MaryAnn and keep her in Utah? How did you suppose MaryAnn's father became HIV-positive? Did you think that he and Lee were lovers, or that her father contracted the virus by accident during surgery? Should it even matter how he became infected? Do you think MaryAnn cared how he became infected? Why or why not?

There are a million questions that we could ask, but one stands out from all the rest. How much must MaryAnn's father love her to send her away at a time when he needed her the very most?

Jocelyn

"For many kids, having a gay parent is nothing but one big cover-up, a giant secret. How would you like it if your mom was politically active and a gay minister? As you can see, secrecy is not an option in my life. I'm fifteen years old, date cute guys, and in addition to everything else, my mom has AIDS. What's even worse, my maternal grandmother is fighting for custody of me when my mom dies. She says she won't let me continue living with Dee, my mom's lover, and Holly, her twelve-year-old daughter and my 'sister'. So if you think life is rough for you, try walking in my shoes for a month.

"My life story is pretty interesting, and from the very beginning it took a lot of unexpected twists. My mother suspected most of her life that she was gay, but her parents were extremely prejudiced and she knew better than to talk to them about her feelings. They hated whites, Catholics, Democrats, hillbillies, doctors, and the list could go on and on. Basically, they hated anyone and everyone who was different from them or who disagreed with their opinions. How did my mother, Rosemary, ever turn out to be as loving and accepting as she is? I guess miracles do happen.

"There was one time in Mom's life, though, when she thought her parents had mellowed a little bit. She came home from college and told them that she was pregnant.

Her father said, 'Rosemary, I want to know who the father is. He has to do the right thing and marry you.' Of course, she never told him that she had made a deal with one of her gay male friends and become pregnant by him. Mom wanted to choose my father, and in her opinion Kevin had all the right genes. So my grandparents said she could live with them **until** they saw her on television in a gay march on Washington, carrying a placard that read, LESBIANS HAVE THE RIGHT TO BE PARENTS TOO. Needless to say, they threw her out of the house, less than a month before I was born.

"Dee was kind of Mom's 'knight in shining armor.' They met at the Women's Clinic where I was born. No one was there to coach her through the delivery, as she had moved as far away from her parents as she could. That wasn't very smart, but she did it anyway. When her parents said, 'Rosemary, pack your bags and get the hell out of here. As far as we're concerned, we never want to see you or that bastard child ever again,' she believed them and got out. Unfortunately, she left a lot of good friends who would have stood by her. But Mom is hard-headed, just like me, and she moved all the way to San Diego.

"Finding a place to live or a job in San Diego wasn't easy, especially for a single mother with a newborn. For a while, we lived with one of Dee's friends, an elderly woman named Mrs. Peterson. She loved babies, and she took care of me while Mom worked at the Center for Women's Studies and Services. Meanwhile, Dee frequently visited with us after work. One Sunday, Dee asked Mom if she would like to attend the gay church. Mom said yes, and the three of us attended a non-denominational Christian church called Anchor Ministries. Our lives were never to be the same after that Sunday.

"We moved into Dee's house three months before her baby was due. Holly was born two weeks prematurely, but she was healthy and beautiful. As a three-year-old, I was both excited about my new 'baby doll' and jealous. The problem about who was whose mother didn't exist in our household. After Mom became an ordained minister, she did missionary work in Africa for six months. During that time, Dee assumed all of the parenting responsibilities in the house. Two years later, Mom returned to Africa for another six months to minister to the sick and poor. She sent me postcards and letters, and I was very proud of her missionary work, but I was lonely too. As a teenager, I wanted and needed my mother. When she returned from her second stay in Africa, my mother said she was done traveling for a while; she had missed me very much and was bone tired.

"Discovering new places to eat on weekends was a favorite pastime with the four of us. We took turns deciding what we would look for on any given weekend. Mom's favorite meal was breakfast, mine was lunch, and Dee and Holly enjoyed desserts the most. On the morning we were to find a new breakfast shop, Mom was too tired to get out of bed. Dee had been worried about her weight loss but said nothing to me. By the time we got her to the emergency room, her temperature was 104 degrees. When Dee mentioned that Mom had been in Africa, they quarantined her right away. The specialists thought she had some rare tropical disease. It took four days in the hospital before they told us the diagnosis; my mom had AIDS.

"My mind raced when I heard the news. How could she have gotten AIDS? She might be lesbian, but she was also monogamous and a minister. I knew she didn't abuse drugs, and she wasn't bisexual. Did she receive tainted blood somehow when she had knee surgery? Was her surgeon infected and she didn't know it? Maybe the hospital report was in error. But wait, what had I read about the number of AIDS cases in Africa? Surely she wasn't exposed to the virus by the very people she was trying to help? Was it possible that my mother would never see me graduate from high school or college? Was it possible that she would never see me marry or hold her own grandchildren? What kind of cruel joke was God playing? My mother was a minister who helped the sick; she couldn't die!

"That first trip to the hospital was just one of many to come. Mom is not only HIV-positive, but she also is symptomatic. My mother, Rosemary Blaylock, is no longer the vibrant, joyous person she used to be. Instead, she is wasting away in front of all of us. Holly cries almost every night before she goes to sleep. I hear Mom and Dee crying softly as they lie in bed talking in hushed voices. I, Jocelyn Blaylock, am angry at the world for how they talk about PWAs, People With AIDS; don't they know they are talking about my mother?

"Just in case you're feeling sorry for me, I've saved the best part of the story for last. Mom wrote about her story, and it was published in some religious digest to which her parents subscribe. When they read that she was dying of AIDS and I had no other relatives, they got in touch with Mom at work. Can you believe that my grandparents want me to live with them after my mother dies? I've never even met the people; why should I live with them now? My mother thanked them politely, but said no. Three days later, a lawyer sent Mom a certified letter saying that they were petitioning the courts for custody. Not only was my mother going to die, but these strangers wanted to take me away from Dee and Holly.

"Do you know what I do every night now? I pray that Mom will live until my eighteenth birthday. If she does, my maternal grandparents can't take me away from my family. It's not important **how** she got the disease, she just has it. Whether or not Mom sees me graduate or get married is no longer important either. I just want to be by her side when she dies and hold her hand. When I came into this world, my mom was alone. I don't want her to be alone when she leaves this world, and I don't want Dee to be the only one there. Please God, let my mom live a little bit longer!"

How do you feel about Jocelyn's story? Do you think her mother made a mistake in moving to San Diego? Why do the maternal grandparents suddenly want Jocelyn to live with them? If you were Jocelyn, how would you feel about these grandparents? As the coparent for fifteen years, how does Dee feel? Should she have the legal right to continue parenting Jocelyn? If you were the judge in this case, would you rule that it was in Jocelyn's or Holly's "best interest" to split up the family? Have you figured out the Catch-22 in this situation?

We started this chapter by defining a Catch-22 as a situation in which there is no obvious solution and no real winner. Parenting is a gamble and a risk, even under the best of circumstances. When you add another unknown variable, such as a gay life-style, you or your gay parent may be caught in situations like the ones you have just read. Maybe you have more in common with your gay parent than you thought?

CHAPTER 6

The New Gay

Frontier

Webster defines frontier as "any new or in-
completely investigated field of learning." Why
have we called this chapter "The New Gay
Frontier"? Unlike in the past, when a person married,
had children, divorced, and then acknowledged his or her
homosexuality, individuals are now acknowledging their
homosexuality first, marrying whenever and wherever
possible, and then planning their children very carefully.
Medical technology, which includes artificial insemination,
in vitro fertilization, and surrogate motherhood, has
enabled gay men and lesbians to have their own biological
children. As you can see, gay families are venturing into
uncharted waters. There are no norms to follow with this
new wave of children, and gay parents are holding their
breath as their children reach early adolescence. Try to
put yourself in the place of the following people.

Bubba

As a fifth grader, Bubba was considered one of the best athletes in the school. He could run faster and throw a ball farther than anyone else, including all of the sixth graders. His talents were definitely outside the classroom. Bubba's father was a highway patrolman and well respected by the community. That is, until Garth moved in with them three years ago. Unlike his father, who was over six feet tall, wore a uniform and carried a gun, and could win a fight with three men against him, Garth worked as a florist. He was five feet six and weighed no more than 145 pounds. The worst part for Bubba, though, was that Garth picked him up from school at least once a week. Invariably, his classmates taunted him unmercifully the next day. Bubba tried to ignore the names they called Garth, but when they started to attack his father's relationship with Garth, Bubba ended up in the principal's office for fighting. After the third fight, the principal called his father for a conference. Bubba had no idea what he should tell the two men behind closed doors.

His father arrived for the conference promptly. Mr. Johnson, the principal, asked Bubba's father if he knew that his son had gotten in three fights in less than six weeks, and he said yes. Mr. Johnson asked Bubba if there was some problem that he was unaware of, and that was all the prodding Bubba needed. He told his father and Mr. Johnson that his life was miserable now that Garth lived with them. The kids called his father, Garth, and even him "fag" all the time. No one chose him for any of the athletic teams, and he felt totally alone. He hated Garth and school. Why couldn't his father send Garth away so that life could get back to normal? But even more important, why did his father choose someone like Garth to live with? He hated the position that his father had put him in with his friends.

No one had expected the outburst they received from Bubba. Mr. Johnson had been unaware that Bubba's father was gay. Now he could understand why Bubba got in fights. Bubba was really the victim of his father's sexual orientation. Why did his classmates taunt him about Garth? How would you feel if you were Bubba? What would you have done if someone called your father a fag? Should Garth find a more masculine job? If he did, would it change anyone's opinion of his sexual orientation? If you heard this news from your own son in the principal's office, how would you respond? Would you ask Garth to move out? Is Bubba jealous of Garth's relationship with his father? If you were Mr. Johnson, how would you punish Bubba for fighting now that you know the reason behind it?

THE FAMILY FEUD

Many nongay parents go through the same series of reactions that children go through. These reactions may include shock, resentment, anger, and denial. Unlike a child, the partner may find the disclosure personally threatening and become very defensive. "If only I had been a better lover, would this have happened?" How a person handles his or her own reactions will definitely influence how he or she deals with his or her children.

Various aspects of a person's life determine just what the reactions will be. First, the attitude one's parents took has a great deal to do with how one handles any news. Second, whether or not the nongay partner has had the opportunity to know and be around gay people also influences the reactions. If the gay people you knew were warm and friendly, that would certainly lead to a more positive reaction than if you felt uncomfortable with gay people. Third, a person's religious background is bound to have a bearing on how he or she feels about homosexuals in general. Last, but probably most important, is the person's innate ability to be nonjudgmental. If the basic attitude toward gay people has been negative, the reaction to a spouse's being gay can hardly be expected to be any different. Let's see how Kyle handles the news that his wife is lesbian.

Kyle

Kyle and Hillary had been married for fourteen years. They had been through some tough times, but generally speaking they had a fair marriage. Their personalities couldn't have been more different. Hillary was outgoing, carefree, flexible, and just enjoyed whatever life sent her way. Kyle, on the other hand, was more of an introvert. He was set in his ways and very opinionated. You didn't dare disagree with him. Some of their worst family arguments centered around appropriate discipline for their daughter, Cindy. Hillary basically thought that Kyle was unreasonable. Kyle thought that he was the authority on everything. Hillary worried about Cindy's learning to form her own opinions when she was exposed to such a dominant father.

Hillary had many friends. She was one of those people who never met a stranger. But her closest friend was Lisé. They had met in college as roommates. Then they went their separate ways, but they always kept in touch and visited with each other several times a year. Five years ago, Lisé was transferred by her company to Atlanta, where Hillary worked. They were both ecstatic.

The bond of friendship between them had grown through the years. But once they had the opportunity to spend more time together, it grew by leaps and bounds. Hillary began to be aware of how good it felt when she and Lisé touched. There was a special feeling when they hugged that she had never felt before. What was this all about? After more than a year of acknowledging and talking about these feelings, it was obvious to both of them that they were in love.

Kyle was totally unaware of the change in his relationship with his wife. All he knew was that they spent a lot of time together, but now it usually included Lisé. You can imagine his reaction when Hillary told him that she loved Lisé. He went into an absolute rage and threatened to kill her if she didn't end the relationship. He wasn't about to have his friends find out that his wife was a dyke! The gossip around town would ruin his career. Kyle continued to be abusive, and Hillary moved out and filed for divorce.

Meanwhile, Kyle did everything in his power to poison Cindy's mind about her mother. He called Hillary filthy names, told Cindy that God would surely punish her mother for being lesbian, and even said that if Cindy chose to live with her mother, she would also become lesbian and go to hell for it.

Cindy was terrified by her father and confused. She didn't really understand why this choice of her mother's was so awful. After all, Lisé was a good person who had a big heart. But, Cindy also loved her father and couldn't believe he would tell her this if it wasn't true.

In spite of his personal feeling, was Kyle being a good father in trying to alienate Cindy from her mother?

Whose best interest did he really have at heart? Should he have been able to set aside his own prejudice and support Cindy's relationship with her mother until she was old enough to form her own opinion? What would you want your father to do?

If you were Hillary, would you have terminated your relationship with Lisé when Kyle threatened to kill you? How would you overcome the negative ideas that Kyle put in Cindy's mind? Will Cindy ever be able to acknowledge Lisé as a good human being, or will she always associate Lisé with her parents' divorce? As Lisé, what are your biggest obstacles in this relationship?

WORLDS APART

Most people would place a family with a gay parent and a family with a heterosexual parent at opposite ends of the spectrum. Amazingly, however, if the two are closely examined, there are many similarities. The bottom line is that the parenting task of a gay parent largely parallels the task of any single parent. The goal of each should be the same: to be the very best parent he or she can be. If that in fact takes place, no one in either situation could blame the sexual orientation of the parent for a child's inability to adjust. Gay parents are very much aware of society's attack on their life-style, and if indeed they are good parents, they simply work harder to prepare you.

The similarities as well as the differences of these two life-styles are very much part of the next scene. Let's see if you can spot the similarities; the differences are probably easier to identify.

Two Families

Janice is a single parent. Her husband deserted her when Todd was only two years old. Times were tough then, but not nearly as hard as they became when she was left on her own to raise her son. Juggling her job, day care, money, and very little support from her family and friends, she wondered often about her ability to be a good parent. Luckily, she found a neat little apartment in a nice section of town that was within her range financially. Another advantage was that it was near both her job and the day-care center for Todd.

The early years of adjustment were difficult, but she had a million wonderful memories of Todd's preschool days. When he entered school, it became harder for her to manage. The school had many functions that she wanted to attend; however, she couldn't always afford a baby-sitter. When Janice *was* able to attend, she was welcomed with open arms by the teachers and other parents. This was really the first time she had felt supported by anyone since her husband's desertion.

Like most boys, Todd wanted to participate in Cub Scouts, Little League, and the swim team. There was just no way to juggle all of these activities as a single parent, so Janice told him to choose the one he wanted to do the most. Little League it was!

They were both excited when they went to the sporting goods store to buy his uniform. Todd tried on the shirt, pants, socks, shoes, and cap . He tried to get her to buy cleats, but she said he was too young. He was very proud of the way he looked in his uniform. Then the salesman reminded Janice that the League rules required all boys to wear a protective cup to prevent genital injuries. Todd began asking what it was and why he had to wear one.

Janice couldn't help but think about how much a father would have helped now. First of all, she hadn't known about the rule. Second, she didn't know if one size fit everyone. And third, she didn't know how to explain it to Todd in the middle of a crowded store. She did not want him to feel her uneasiness or to think that it was something unnatural. She simply was not prepared to handle this as a parent.

We next focus on Alana, who lives with her gay father, Rob. Her mother died when Alana was in first grade. Fortunately, she and her father had always been very close. Their relationship helped Alana deal with her mother's death. She knew that her mother had been a loving person and that many people loved her. That was very comforting to Alana. Her mother's life insurance policy eliminated what could have been a tremendous financial problem. However, her father was very careful with the money and always reminded Alana of the cost of a college education.

One of the things Alana had trouble understanding was why she and her father moved so much. Was he just restless? Didn't he know what he wanted in an apartment? The only thing that made all the moving bearable was that his brothers and friends were always there to help them move. In fact, her father's brothers and friends were always there whenever they were needed.

Alana's father felt very comfortable attending events with and for her. But she could never understand why it was so hard to blend in with the families of her friends. It seemed as if any group dispersed when they attempted to join it. Was it because she didn't have a mother? Alana desperately wanted them to know this dear person who had stood so firmly by her.

The most trying time for Alana and her father came when she was in the sixth grade. She had been instructed in health class about menstruation, but with no sisters or mother, she had no "in house" knowledge of what it was like. She was dressing for the end-of-the-year school dance when she became aware that she had started her period. What could she do? Her friends were picking her up in half an hour. She couldn't drive, and there were no supplies in the house. The only choice was to tell her dad. Oh brother, she certainly hoped he could handle this!

Actually, it turned out to be one of the moments with him that she would always remember. When she said, "Dad, I've started my period," he simply came over and held her close for a long time. Then he said, "I'll take care of it now, but I want to talk with you about it tomorrow." He asked Alana if she was okay and left for the store.

Reflecting on the lives of these two families, we see much that is the same and much that is different. Let's look at the likenesses first. The most obvious is that both children were being raised by a single parent. Each parent felt equally uncomfortable dealing with a personal issue with the opposite-sex child. No matter how different the obstacles were, both parents ran into roadblocks in trying to raise a child alone. Most important, both parents were totally committed to the welfare and happiness of their child and met those needs first.

Financially, the two families were very different. Todd's mother had trouble making ends meet, whereas the death of Alana's mother provided financial security for Alana and her father. When it came to support groups, Rob certainly had more going for him than Janice did. The reception at school functions, however, was in direct contrast. Janice was received with open arms, whereas

Rob was ostracized. Why was Janice able to enjoy a comfortable apartment for a long time but Rob constantly had to move? In case you haven't figured it out, Rob's neighbors complained about his sexual orientation. If the landlord was compassionate, Rob and Alana were given thirty days' notice; otherwise, they had to pack and move in ten days. Fortunately, Alana was still too young to realize that her father was gay and was being discriminated against.

What is important here is not the problems each parent faced, but **how** they faced them. The total commitment that both Janice and Rob showed for their children is unquestionable. Did Rob's sexual orientation interfere with his parenting skills? Did your parents do a better job than Rob? Could you?

THE DATING GAME

Coparenting is probably one of the most challenging aspects that can face a family. Whether you are speaking of a gay couple or a heterosexual couple, achieving harmony in this situation is a formidable task. Introducing a new person into an existing family structure takes patience, time, and perseverance.

There is no doubt that the gay couple have far fewer choices in making the transition. If the goal of the gay parent is to have his or her partner accepted as a friend first and a lover second, they cannot be seen in public as a couple. Our prejudiced society would label the couple queer, unnatural, or immoral, and no one would take the time to discover whether or not this new partner was a kind and loving human being. The stereotypes assigned to the relationship would never allow children, family members, or friends to see his or her positive characteristics, and this person would never be accepted as a member of the family. In addition, many positive feelings you had about your parent might also be jeopardized.

In contrast, a heterosexual couple is encouraged by society to display their commitment to each other. Walks in the park, bike rides, Saturday night movies, and church on Sunday are all acceptable avenues for a heterosexual couple to begin the assimilation of a new family member. These avenues of spending time together and getting to know each other are simply not accessible to a gay couple with the very same intentions.

Another area of difficulty and inequality is that of affection. One of the most powerful demonstrations of love and caring for another is the open display of affection. How many heterosexual couples who are dating think twice about holding hands with their partner? For a gay couple who are dating, that is rarely even a remote possibility. It is simply understood that there can be no open display of affection.

Can your gay parent be frequently affectionate with someone of the same gender and find you accepting, or does it alienate you? Once again, your age plays a significant role in acceptance. To the younger child, it would be a natural expression of love and caring. To an older child, it might seem perverse or threatening, especially if you are the same gender as your gay parent. As you can see, the boundaries of interaction are more confined and the choices more limited for gay parents trying to build a family.

Given that situation, it is obvious that to achieve the same goal—a stable, accepting, and loving family—the gay couple must work much harder than the heterosexual couple. A great deal more thought has to go into appropriate ways of relating in front of children, family members, friends, and society. It is awfully hard to do that and be spontaneous at the same time. Let's see how Vanessa tiptoed through this maze.

Vanessa

Vanessa has a fourteen-year-old son, Sandy, whom she adopted when he was three years old. He had already been in and out of several foster homes and was the victim of physical abuse and neglect. Vanessa has been working very hard both at her job and at being a single parent. Two years ago, at a business meeting in Seattle, she met Luisa. Luisa's job was very similar to hers, but in another branch. They talked about the similarities and differences of working in different parts of the city. Vanessa felt comfortable with Luisa right away. She was so easy to talk to, and they had a lot of common interests. They agreed to get together for lunch the next week, and from that time their relationship slowly grew to heights neither had ever imagined possible. At the end of a two-year, long-distance relationship, each of them acknowledged a commitment to spend the rest of her life with the other.

Luisa was first introduced to Sandy as a business acquaintance. Sandy knew that the two of them got together fairly often for lunch, dinner, or shows, but soon Luisa began spending more time at their house. His mom was sure easier to get along with since she met Luisa. He even felt comfortable asking Luisa's advice on things he couldn't talk to his mother about. In many ways, he felt as if he had two parents; what a strange, but also comforting feeling. Somewhere within him remained the memory of the abuse, violence, and neglect he had received at the hands of his biological parents. The foster homes were okay, but there was something missing in all of those homes—love. All Sandy knew was that he liked the atmosphere in the house when Luisa was around. There was a sense of warmth, happiness, and acceptance that he never remembered before.

At the same time Sandy was enjoying these feelings, Vanessa and Luisa were going through much stress and anxiety plotting their every move in Sandy's best interest. They knew what their goal was—to have Sandy accept them as a couple. He had long ago accepted Luisa as a special person. How could they demonstrate their deep love for each other and not threaten or offend Sandy? Where, exactly, were their boundaries?

They progressed slowly, sharing the preparation of many meals, sitting down together and eating, and even helping Sandy clean up. They always had music playing and acknowledged special songs that they liked. They talked openly about occasions they would be sharing, both professional and personal. How would they know when Sandy recognized the bond of love between them? Would it be in their best interest to display affection for each other before they told Sandy the truth? Considering his age, did they even have to tell him the truth?

Vanessa and Luisa had been very careful to make most of their public get-togethers business-oriented. They did go to a concert or movie occasionally, but they always erred on the cautious side so that no one would label them a couple. The intimate time they spent together was always at Luisa's. Neither was willing to risk losing Sandy.

Each of these women desperately missed the pleasure of walking hand in hand on the beach, putting an arm around the other in the movie theater, or gazing lovingly across the table in a restaurant. Think about the pressure this concealment puts on a relationship. How can you be real and not real at the same time? Do you think that a committed heterosexual couple would ever even consider trying so hard to make things work? Is not the willingness to do so evidence of the gay parent's devotion to the child first and the partner second? Do Vanessa and Luisa not deserve admiration, respect, and support? Would you be willing to go through the sacrifices and turmoil that they did for their child? Think about it. How would you have behaved if you were Vanessa and Luisa? Why didn't Luisa just move in with Vanessa after a year of dating? How would you have felt if you were Sandy? Would you have wanted Luisa to move in? Would you have had the courage to confront your own mother about her relationship with Luisa? Why or why not? Do you think that Vanessa and Luisa should hide their relationship from Sandy and wait until he leaves for college before they live together? If this were a heterosexual couple, would you have given them the same advice? Why or why not?

JEOPARDY

In a heterosexual household, it doesn't matter what parents do behind closed doors. The behavior of gay parents, however—sexual or nonsexual—is scrutinized by everyone. It appears that *it does matter* what they do behind closed doors. In order to arm their children for verbal and sometimes physical abuse by others, gay parents face the decision of self-disclosure. You have read how varied are the reactions of both adults and children. Every time a gay parent acknowledges his or her sexual orientation, he or she runs the risk of losing his or her child forever. There are no models for children of gay parents to follow. You may be struggling right now with your own feelings about a gay parent. It is important for you to realize that you are not alone in this time of confusion.

Gay parents hope they have taught their children that *loving someone of the same gender is just another way of loving.* If gay parents have accomplished this task, their children will hate them for only a short time, just like any other adolescent growing up. The New Gay Frontier is a reality, and how well we tame it is up to you!

Epilogue

Of all the issues that having a gay parent raises, the one that usually takes longest to deal with is your own sexual identity. Let's address these concerns one last time.

First, homosexuality is not inherited! Second, all children go through stages of same-sex experimentation. Childhood homosexual activity is healthy and a normal part of growing up. Third, heterosexual dating during adolescence is **not** a form of denial. The fact that your parent is gay does not mean that you will be gay. Only one in ten young people is gay, and dating is also a normal developmental stage. Fourth, try not to second-guess yourself if you break up with someone you are dating. Rather than convincing yourself that you broke up because you wanted to date someone of the same gender, focus on the fact that you broke up with this person because the qualities you were looking for in a partner were missing. Focus on the person's behavior and personal characteristics before you question the gender. And last, there is no guarantee that in forty or fifty years you won't acknowledge your own feelings of homosexuality. But until then, figure out how you want to live. As long as you're not hurting anyone else and you feel it is right for you— do it.

Having started this book by tracing the evolution of the American family, it is only fitting that we end by addressing the family once again. The family in the 1990s has a complex cast of characters. Intact families are becoming rare, and blended or stepfamilies are becoming the norm. The parallels between stepfamilies and gay families are too significant to ignore. The cast of characters after a divorce might include:

Biological mother and stepfather
Biological father and stepmother
Maternal grandparents
Paternal grandparents
Stepfather's parents = your new stepgrandparents
Stepmother's parents = your new stepgrandparents

With a few minor changes, the cast of characters with a gay parent looks remarkably the same. Try to insert your own family into this model:

Lesbian biological mother and female partner (new stepparent)
Biological father and stepmother
Maternal grandparents
Paternal grandparents
Female partner's parents = your new stepgrandparents
Stepmother's parents = your new stepgrandparents

Parents are not sculptors who can mold a world that accepts their children for who they are, including all their strengths and weaknesses. Instead, parents give love and nurturance, are sensitive to your needs and abilities, and provide guidance and limits. When parents do those things, they are enabling you to become the best person you can be. If your parent does those things for you, should it really matter what his or her sexual orientation is?

Bibliography

Alpert, H. *We Are Everywhere: Writings By and About Lesbian Parents*. Freedom. CA.: Crossing Press, 1988.

Barret, R., and Robinson, B. *Gay Fathers*. Massachusetts: D.C. Heath and Company (Lexington Books), 1990.

Beiber, I. "A Discussion of Homosexuality: The Ethical Challenge." *Journal of Consulting and Clinical Psychology*, 1976, 44, 163–166.

Bell, A.P., and Weinberg, M.S. *Homosexualities*. New York: Simon & Schuster, 1978.

Bell, A.P., Weinberg, M.S., and Hammersmith, S.K. *Sexual Preference: Its Development in Men and Women*. Bloomington, IL: Indiana University Press, 1981.

Calderone, M., and Johnson, E. *The Family Book About Sexuality*. New York: Harper & Row, 1981.

Calderone, M., and Ramey, J. *Talking with Your Child About Sex*. New York: Random House, 1982.

Cramer, D. "Gay Parents and Their Children: A Review of Research and Practical Implications." *Journal of Counseling and Development*, 64 (1986):504–507.

Curtis, W., ed. *Revelations: A Collection of Gay Men's Coming Out Stories*. Boston: Alyson, 1988.

Dank, B.M. "Coming out in the Gay World." *Psychiatry*. 1971, 34, 180–197.

Gagnon, J.H. "Sexuality and Sexual Learning in the Child." *Psychiatry*, 1965, 28, 212–228.

Geller, T., ed. *Bisexuality: A Reader and Resourcebook*. Ojai, CA: Times Change Press, 1990.

Gelman, D. "Born or Bred: The Origins of Homosexuality," *Newsweek*, February 24, 1992, 46–53.

Goldstein, R. "The Gay Family." *Voices*, 11:27 (1986):21–24.

Gordon, S., and Snyder, C.W. *Personal Issues in Human Sexuality: A Guidebook for Better Sexual Health*. Boston: Allyn and Bacon, 1989.

Harry, J., and DeVall, B. *The Social Organization of Gay Males*. New York: Praeger, 1978.

Hutchins, L., and Kaahumanu, L., eds. *By Any Other Name*. Boston: Alyson Publications, 1991.

Holtzen, D.W., and Agresti, A. "Parental Responses to Gay and Lesbian Children." *Journal of Social and Clinical Psychology*, 9:3 (Fall 1990):390–399.

Jay, K., and Young, A. *The Gay Report*. New York: Summit Books, 1979.

Kaplan, H.S., and Sager, C.J. "Sexual Patterns at Different Ages." *Medical Aspects of Human Sexuality*, 1971, 6, 10–23.

Kinsey, A., et al. *Sexual Behavior in the Human Male*. Philadelphia: W.B. Saunders, 1948.

Kinsey, A., et al. *Sexual Behavior in the Human Female*. Philadelphia: W.B. Saunders, 1953.

Levitt, E.E., and Klassen, A. "Public Attitudes Toward Homosexuality." *Journal of Homosexuality*, 1(1), 1974, 29–45.

Loicano, D. "Sex Identity Issues Among Black Americans: Racism, Homophobia, and the Need for Validation." Journal of Counseling and Development, 68:1 (September–October 1989): 21–25.

Marmor, J., ed. *Homosexual Behavior*. New York: Basic Books, 1980.

Masters, W.H., and Johnson, V.E. *Homosexuality in Perspective*. Boston: Little, Brown, 1979.

Miller, P.Y., and Simon, W. "The Development of Sexuality in Adolescence." In J. Adelson (ed.), *Handbook of Adolescent Psychology*. New York: Wiley, 1980.

Money, J., and Tucker, P. *Sexual Signatures*. Boston: Little, Brown, 1975, 91–92.

Nyberg, K. L., and Alston, J.P. "An Analysis of Public Attitudes

Toward Homosexual Behavior." *Journal of Homosexuality*, 2(2), 1977, 99–107.

Peplau, L.A. "What Homosexuals Want." *Psychology Today*, March 1981, 28–38.

Pogrebin, L. *Growing Up Free: Raising Your Child in the 80's.* New York: McGraw-Hill, 1980.

Rafkin, L. *Different Mothers: Sons and Daughters of Lesbians Talk About Their Lives.* Pittsburgh: Cleis Press, Inc., 1990.

Rosen, D.H. *Lesbianism: A Study of Female Homosexuality.* Springfield, IL: Charles C. Thomas Company, 1974.

Spada, J. *The Spada Report.* New York: Signet Books, 1979.

Tripp, C. *The Homosexual Matrix.* New York: McGraw-Hill, 1974.

Warren, C. *Identity and Community in the Gay World.* New York: Wiley, 1974.

Weinberg, M.S., and Williams, C, *Male Homosexuals: Their Preferences and Adaptations.* New York: Oxford Press, 1974.

Zinik, G. "Identity Conflict or Adaptive Flexibility? Bisexuality Reconsidered." *Journal of Homosexuality*, 1985, 11, 7–19.

Appendix

RELIGIOUS ORGANIZATIONS

The following religious organizations try to stop homophobia and promote equality for lesbian, gay, and bisexual people within the religious community.

Affirmation: United Methodists for Lesbian/Gay Concerns
P.O. Box 1021
Evanston, IL 60204

American Baptists Concerned
872 Erie Street
Oakland, CA 94610
(415) 465-8652, 465-2778

Dignity (Catholic)
1500 Massachusetts Avenue, NW
Washington, DC 20005
(202) 861-0017

Friends for Lesbian and Gay Concerns (Quaker)
P.O. Box 222
Sunneytown, PA 18084
(215) 234-8424

Lutherans Concerned/North America
P.O. Box 10461, Fort Dearborn Station
Chicago, IL 60610-0461

New Jewish Agenda
 64 Fulton Street
 New York, NY 10038
 (22) 227-5885

New Ways Ministry (Catholic)
 4012 29th Street
 Mt. Rainier, MD 20712
 (301) 277-566674

Presbyterians for Lesbian/Gay Concerns
 P.O. Box 38
 New Brunswick, NJ 09903-0038

Seventh-Day Adventist Kinship International, Inc.
 P.O. Box 3840
 Los Angeles, CA 90078-3840
 (213) 876-2076

Universal Fellowship of Metropolitan Community Churches
 5300 Santa Monica Boulevard
 Los Angeles, CA 90029
 (213) 464-5100

ORGANIZATIONS AND PROJECTS

National Gay/Lesbian Crisis Line
1-800-22-7044
NY, AK, HW: (212) 529-1604

Mon.-Fri. 3:00–10:00 p.m. E.S.T.
Sat. 1:00–5:00 p.m.

Pen-Friend
A project of the National Gay Alliance for Young Adults
(NGAYA)
   P.O. Box 190426
   Dallas, TX 75219-0426
   Pen-Friend is a pen pal coordination service for gay
      adolescents and young adults.

Letter Exchange Project
Alyson Publications
   40 Plympton Street
   Boston, MA 02118
   (617) 542-5679

An organization similar to Pen-Friend.

Federation of Parents and Friends of Lesbians and Gays
(Parents FLAG)
   P.O. Box 20308
   Denver, Co. 80220
   (303) 321-2270

A national self-help organization that helps parents and
their gay children understand, love, and communicate
with each other. Local chapters exist.

Annotated Reading List

(**Reading list adapted from** *Booklist*.)

Brett, Catherine. *S.P. Likes A.D.* New York: The Women's Press Ltd.; dist. by Inland, 1989.

S.P. doesn't know why she is attracted to a female classmate (A.D.), but she worries about the intensity of her feelings. Then S.P. gets to know two of her mother's friends, whose close relationship gives her a role model for love.

Bunn, Scott. *Just Hold On.* New York: Delacorte, 1982.

Stephen and Charlotte, drawn together as they deal with their troubled parents (Stephen's father is an alcoholic; Charlotte is an incest victim), become part of a close group of friends who accept Stephen and Rolf when they become lovers.

Childress, Alice. *Those Other People.* New York: Putnam, 1989.

A contemporary novel told from a variety of viewpoints: from the gay teenager who has left home to find himself, to the black teenager whose family has just moved to an all-white neighborhood, to the young woman who has a reputation for being easy, to the high school teacher who thinks he's justified in copping a feel. All have their own voices and their own very definite opinions of "those other people."

Garden, Nancy. *Annie on My Mind*. New York: Farrar, Straus & Giroux, 1982.

When Liza and Annie, two New York City high school seniors, meet, they are immediately drawn to each other. Although both young women face conflicts in accepting their feelings of attraction, the story captures the magic and intensity of first love.

Hall, Lynn. *Sticks and Stones*. Ohio: Follett, 1977.

Tom is welcomed as a newcomer at a rural Iowa high school until his friendship with a boy who is rumored to be gay stigmatizes him in the eyes of the community. The author paints a stark and thought-provoking picture of homophobia in this novel about the motivation and destructive power of gossip.

Homes, A.M. *Jack*. New York: Macmillan, Inc., 1989.

Jack is a witty, tough-talking son of divorced parents whose life is disrupted when his father comes out to him. His anger eventually dissipates as he adjusts to his father's life-style.

Kerr, M.E. *I'll Love You When You're More Like Me*. New York: Harper, 1977.

Three young people face problems as they confront parental and societal expectations: Wally is at odds with his father, Sabra is trying to ease out from under her mother's domination, and Charlie is the town outcast for telling his family he "believed he preferred boys to girls."

Kerr, M.E. *Nightkites*. New York: Harper, 1986.

Erick is seventeen when he learns his older brother, Pete, is gay and has AIDS. The negative impact on Erick and his parents is considerable. But Pete and Erick have a good relationship in a story in which the villain is not only the disease, but also the mindless fear it raises in the community.

Klein, Norma. *Breaking Up*. New York: Random/Pantheon, 1980.

Ali Rose lives in New York City with her mother, her brother, and her mother's friend, Peggy. While spending the summer with her father and his new wife, Ali is confronted with the fact that her mother and Peggy are more than "just good friends." Her father's threatened custody battle is both alarming and realistic.

Klein, Norma. *My Life as a Body*. New York: Alfred A. Knopf, 1987.

Augie is a shy, intelligent girl who falls in love with Sam, a wheelchair-bound classmate. During the span of this novel Augie, Sam, and Augie's best friend, Claudia, who's "known since she was five that she was gay," leave home for college and continue their journey toward adulthood.

Klein, Norma. *Now That I Know*. New York: Bantam, 1988.

Her parents' shared custody arrangement is fine with Nina until her father tells her that he is gay and his lover is moving in with him. Though she worries about sharing her father's attention and about the social stigma of having a gay parent, Nina is finally able to sort out her own feelings and reconcile with her father.

Koertge, Ron. *The Arizona Kid*. New York: Avon, 1988.

Sixteen-year-old Billy spends the summer in Tucson working at a racetrack and getting to know his Uncle Wes, whose complete acceptance of his own gay identity and his warm regard for his nephew come through strongly, as does life in a gay community facing the AIDS crisis.

L'Engle, Madeleine. *A House Like a Lotus*. New York: Farrar, Straus & Giroux, 1984.

Suffering the pangs of adolescent gawkiness, Polly O'Keefe is made to feel confident and special by Max, a beautiful and talented artist friend of Polly's family, who lives nearby with Ursula, her companion of thirty years. When Polly learns that Max and Ursula are lovers, the plot becomes something of a soap opera. Still, Polly's maturation in the course of the novel is well done.

Meyer, Carolyn. *Elliott and Win*. New York: Macmillan/ Collier, 1986.

From the moment Win first walks into Elliott's house, he is certain that their relationship as "Big Brothers" is going to be a disaster—Elliott cares nothing for team sports, serves gazpacho for lunch, and doesn't even own a television. Though Elliott fits a number of gay male stereotypes, his sexual orientation is never defined, nor is it necessary to do so, since Win finds that forging friendships is more important than fitting the traditional masculine mold.

Reading, J.P. *Bouquets for Brimbal*. New York: Harper, 1980.

Macy Beacon and Annie Brimbal have been best friends for years, but when they go off to summer stock theater after high school graduation, their lives begin to separate. Annie becomes romantically involved with another actress—and Macy finds she must accept Annie's new relationship if their friendship is to continue.

Rees, David. *Out of the Winter Gardens*. New York: Olive Branch Press; dist. by Inland, 1984.

Sixteen-year-old Mike has not seen his father since he was very young. When his father invites him for a visit, Mike learns almost immediately that his father is gay, and the three-week visit changes Mike's life—not in "turning him gay" as his mother feared but in establishing a warm father-son relationship.

Scoppettone, Sandra. *Trying Hard to Hear You.* New York: Harper, 1974.

Camilla tells the story of her close-knit summer stock theater crowd, and of Jeff and Phil, who were part of the crowd—until they fell in love. Though most of their peers react with confusion and hostility, Camilla progresses from prejudice to acceptance.

Shannon, George. *Unlived Affections.* New York: Harper, 1989.

After Willy's grandmother/guardian dies, he finds a hidden collection of old letters from his father to his mother. The story is told through the letters and is skillfully done. Willy eventually becomes acquainted with the father he never knew, a man who had come to terms with his gay sexual preference at the cost of his marriage.

Ure, Jean. *The Other Side of the Fence.* New York: Delacorte, 1986.

Richard leaves home after a quarrel with his parents and picks up hitchhiker Bonny, a tart-tongued working-class teen who is also running away. Each helps the other face and overcome parental and societal disapproval. Richard returns to his male lover, while Bonny returns to her foster parents. The reader sees that people of different backgrounds—both in sexual orientation and class—can enrich each other's lives.

Wersba, Barbara. *Crazy Vanilla*. New York: Harper, 1986.

At age fourteen, Tyler feels estranged from his family. His father is distant, his mother is an alcoholic, and his brother Cameron has been banished from the family for being gay. When Tyler first meets Mitzi Gerrard, he is immediately put off by her brash manner and loud mouth. However, their mutual interest in photography draws them together. Tyler is finally able to talk to someone about his feelings for his family and rebuilds the relationship with his brother.

Wersba, Barbara. *Just Be Gorgeous*. New York: Harper, 1988.

A New York City teenager is convinced of her own unattractiveness, but a gay teenage waif who supports himself by tap dancing on the street becomes her best friend, companion, and morale-booster, telling her to "just be gorgeous." Both are determined to be true to themselves, and both find enough of what they are looking for to keep them going.

*   *   *

Cohen, Susan and Daniel. *When Someone You Know Is Gay*. New York: M. Evans, 1989.

Written for teens who have a gay friend or relative, the Cohens' self-help book dispels common stereotypes with basic information to promote a better understanding of the gay and lesbian experience.

Index